INQUISITIVE LEADERSHIP

A NEW APPROACH TO CULTIVATING HIGH PERFORMANCE

Frederica A. Peterson, MA, CPC, ACC

© 2026 Frederica A. Peterson. All rights reserved.

No part of this work may be reproduced or utilized in any form, or by any electronic, mechanical, or other means now known or hereafter invented—including xerography, photocopying, recording, or inclusion in any information storage and retrieval system, or for the purpose of training generative artificial intelligence technologies—without the written permission of the publisher.

Inquisitive Leadership: A New Approach to Cultivating High Performance

by Frederica A. Peterson, MA, CPC, ACC

Library of Congress Control Number: 2026900570

ISBN:

978-1-959009-26-9 (eBook)

978-1-959009-30-6 (Paperback)

978-1-959009-31-3 (Hardcover)

Published 2026 in the United States by

Simply Good Press, Montclair, N.J.

The CAPPP Advantage™ Performance Model and all associated frameworks, visuals, and diagnostic architectures presented in this book are original works of the author. Reproduction or distribution without written permission is prohibited.

Cover Art by: Na'Shaun Groover

TABLE OF CONTENTS

I dedicate this book to my late father, retired Montclair Police Captain Auburn E. Peterson. Your leadership and legacy had the greatest impact on my life and paved the way for my own journey as a leader.

Your courage, tenacity and strength, especially during a time when leadership for a Black man was exceptionally challenging, taught me and my sister Lita how to overcome obstacles unapologetically. All the while, you were an incredible mentor and a tireless community advocate.

Being a single parent wasn't easy, yet you were the very definition of a girl-dad. Our small family was my first team . We navigated difficult times together, with you always keeping us safe and leading the way on a road not easily traveled. While things weren't always perfect, you showed us that mistakes were part of leadership, as long as we owned them and kept our heads held high in the face of adversity.

You were a true trailblazer for your generation, yet received only a fraction of the recognition you deserved. My hope is that your legacy will continue to live on through me, in my work and in the leaders I serve. I miss you every day and hope I am still making you proud.

FOREWORD

Over my career I've had the privilege of leading teams through moments of extraordinary challenge and opportunity. One of the most important lessons I've taken is that effective leadership isn't defined by certainty but by the willingness to explore. That's why *Inquisitive Leadership* resonates so deeply with me. Frederica "Kiki" Peterson has captured in her framework what I believe to be the heart of effective leadership: building trust, valuing people, and inspiring purpose.

Expectations placed on leaders have expanded dramatically. Today's workforce demands more than operational expertise. They want leaders who are self-aware, inclusive, adaptable, and courageous enough to navigate hard conversations with honesty and respect. These are not "soft skills." They are business-critical competencies that determine whether teams flourish or fracture — and they directly influence performance, retention, innovation, and trust.

I first met Kiki during a leadership development program where she served as a coach to our peer group. Her approach was refreshingly practical yet deeply human: grounded in connection, curiosity, and growth. Reading this book brought back memories of pivotal moments in my own journey that reflect the five stages of her framework.

Across those moments, one theme stood out: the critical importance of working together as a team toward a shared goal. Teams thrive when collaboration is built on genuine respect, because it's the cornerstone of meaningful work together. When leaders create an environment where every team member feels valued, and authentic relationships can take root, unity becomes a competitive advantage. Even in turbulent times, extraordinary results become possible. At the center of all this lies a powerful lesson: Connection is not optional; it is the foundation of performance.

My experiences taught me that leadership is a journey of curiosity about people, about purpose, and about possibilities. Kiki's CAPPP Advantage™ Framework offers a roadmap for that journey. It is practical, insightful, and deeply relevant for anyone who aspires to lead with impact. Her framework challenges leaders to look inward, listen deeply, and lead with intention.

As you turn the pages of this book, I invite you to reflect on your own leadership story. Ask yourself the questions that matter. Stay curious. And above all, lead in a way that brings out the best in others, because that is where meaningful leadership truly begins.

— Antonio Escalona, Board Member and Former SVP, Emerging Business at PepsiCo Foods North America

ACKNOWLEDGMENTS

First, I give thanks to Christ, the foundation of my life and work, through whom this gift of writing and leadership has been made possible.

This book was shaped by people and communities who challenged me to think more deeply, listen more carefully and remain open to learning, especially when it would have been easier not to.

I am deeply grateful to Elaine Pofeldt, whose editorial rigor and thoughtful challenge strengthened both the framework and the voice of this book. Your insistence on precision and your willingness to push my thinking made *Inquisitive Leadership* better in every way.

Thank you to Jane Tabachnick / Simply Good Press for believing in this work and shepherding it into the world with care and professionalism. Your partnership ensured this book reached the leaders it was written to serve.

I am also grateful to Antonio Escalona for contributing the foreword. Your leadership, perspective, and willingness to lend your voice added depth and credibility, and I am honored by your support.

Special thanks to my nephew, NaShaun, who illustrated the cover. Your cre-ativity brought the spirit of this book to life visually, and it means more than I can express to share my work with you in this way.

This work was shaped profoundly by the leaders who trusted me with their real-world experiences. To my coaching clients, workshop participants, orga-nizational partners, and the teams I led during my corporate career, thank you for your honesty, questions, and willingness to sit with discomfort. Whether learning alongside me or testing these ideas in practice, your experiences informed these pages more than any research ever could. You reinforced my belief that leadership effectiveness is not about level or title, but about practice.

I extend my deepest gratitude to the colleagues and thought partners who challenged my assumptions, engaged me in meaningful dialogue, and provided valuable feedback, which was instrumental in shaping this work. Special thanks to my whitepaper readers: Marielis, Michael, Arthur, Lillian, Leslie, Freda, Antonio, Lisa, and Priya.

My longtime colleague and friend, Joyel Crawford, deserves particular mention for her steady encouragement, belief in this work, and consistent follow-up, which helped me persevere through the long and uncertain process.

Finally, to Riz, the backbone of my business operations, thank you. Your support in keeping me focused and on task, despite my endless projects and creative brainstorms, was essential to seeing this project through to completion. What would I do without you?

I also want to acknowledge my former pastor, Dr. David D. Ireland, who shepherded me for 23 years and was the first to plant the seed that I would write books. Your encouragement and consistent teaching laid a foundation of confidence that continues to shape my leadership journey today.

Finally, to the leaders reading *Inquisitive Leadership*: thank you for choosing curiosity over certainty and growth over comfort. Leadership rooted in inquiry requires courage, the courage to ask better questions, to listen without defensiveness, and to remain open to learning. I hope this book supports you in that practice, and that the impact of your leadership extends far beyond what is written here.

INTRODUCTION

Curiosity has always been my most powerful guide.

Long before I ever led a team or coached an executive, I was a people-watcher. Growing up, I could sit in a park or mall for hours and entertain myself by observing the people around me. I'd create stories about random strangers and what had brought them to the place we shared at that particular moment. I didn't know it at the time, but that habit of wondering about the people around me was helping me develop one of the most valuable leadership skills: curiosity.

Growing up in Montclair, N.J., a very diverse, middle-class community, I was surrounded by friends from all walks of life, and I liked it that way. The more dissimilar someone was from me, the more I wanted to know about them. While many classmates would make fun of "nerdy" kids who didn't fit in, I wanted to get to know them and find out what made them who they were. My curiosity has almost always led to warmth, friendship and a greater understanding of what connected us as people. Even as a high school student, I found energy in connecting with others.

That lifelong passion for connection became the foundation of my career and eventually, this book. For the past 30 years, I've had the opportunity to coach and train hundreds of leaders in the corporate world to help them connect with their people. One truth has stood out: The most effective leaders are not necessarily the most talented and hardworking. They are the most inquisitive.

Many executives and managers, despite their intelligence and drive, are frustrated that they can't unlock the potential, passion and commitment of their teams. Yet they unknowingly limit their own effectiveness by neglecting a single critical skill: effective communication. They manage tasks, emails, and progress reports well, but they don't truly connect with their people. As a result, they unintentionally distance themselves from the very teams they depend on. Oftentimes, this is because they are not exercising their innate curiosity about the people they work with. If you have ever felt like you were working relentlessly to meet your company's goals but experienced the empty feeling of going through the motions, it might be because you aren't fully aware of the many opportunities to exercise your own authentic curiosity in your own workplace. This book will help you tap into that hidden superpower so you can reach your potential as a leader while helping your team to thrive.

True leadership isn't about steering a team from a mountaintop. It's about connecting through genuine, intentional, "knee-to knee" conversations. The bedrock is understanding individual team members—what motivates them, how they think, and what they need to do their best work. When team members feel seen and genuinely cared for, they are more likely to immerse themselves fully in the projects at hand and participate in your workplace culture. Conversely, if they perceive a lack of genuine interest, their engagement will mirror that sentiment. The energy and commitment your team gives will always mirror the effort you put into building these relationships.

This principle sits at the heart of *Inquisitive Leadership*, which is built on decades of experience building and leading high-performing teams, and observing how leaders communicate, connect, and motivate their teams. Inquisitive Leadership is about transforming curiosity into a leadership practice, one that strengthens relationships, creates cultures where individuals can thrive, and ultimately fosters peak performance. This book is designed to help anyone in a position to lead a team, whether you are a new manager looking for ways to connect with your employees, a seasoned leader looking to increase productivity or build confidence as a leader, or an executive looking to build a stronger culture at your company.

But here's the tricky part: Many leaders know authentic communication is important yet find it hard to practice consistently. It can be difficult to stay open and curious while maintaining your authority. It's even harder if your team is spread out across different time zones and cultures. Given the pace of business, it's easy to replace meaningful conversations with quick updates, long email threads, and surface-level discussions. Leaders can end up feeling isolated, and their teams unseen.

The irony is that most leaders already have the talented people they need to succeed. They just haven't learned to unlock their team's potential by asking the right questions. The answers are there, waiting for leaders who are willing to be vulnerable and committed to exercising their own curiosity.

So, how do you do that? It starts with intentional communication, being present, asking questions, and listening carefully. Your job as a leader is not only creating a strategy for the business but also leading the cultural work of the team. As the influential management thinker Peter Drucker was famous for saying, "Culture eats strategy for breakfast," and it is the truth. Culture is built one authentic conversation at a time.

This book will help you understand and master the five crucial stages of *Inquisitive Leadership*: Building Connection and Rapport, Assessing your Team, Valuing People, Understanding Purpose, and Cultivating Performance. It is a practical guidebook to the conversations every leader needs to have and the nonverbal, intuitive skills they must develop to unlock their team's potential.

You'll learn to ask the questions that build trust, alignment, and results while navigating differences across age, gender, culture, education and lived experience. Of course, that journey may not always be comfortable as you immerse yourself in the intricacies of team dynamics in all of their gritty reality. Authentic communication requires vulnerability and an acceptance that you don't have all the answers, or need to. For many of the managers and executives I coach, admitting they don't know something seems like a risky proposition. Most of us reached our current status because of our expertise. However, once we become leaders, our role changes. Our power no longer comes from having all the answers.

It comes from asking the right questions, even when it's uncomfortable—something I call *Courageous Curiosity*. *Courageous Curiosity* is about taking a genuine interest in the perspectives of the individuals on your team, even when this might expose a gap in your knowledge or challenge your assumptions. When you do this consistently, it sets the tone for a culture where curiosity, not fear of being "found out," drives performance.

In practice, *Courageous Curiosity* could mean taking the time to find out that one individual on your team takes lunch every day at noon to study for a new degree, or that another wants to work on a special project in another department where they aspire to work. Understanding some of the daily details of each person's identity outside the context of their role may seem daunting at first glance, but doing so builds connection and trust. It shows you see your team members as people, not just employees. That's where the magic of engagement begins.

As I often advise the leaders I coach, *Courageous Curiosity* is the greatest gift you can give yourself and others. When you apply the principles in this book, you'll find that it isn't just a skill. It's a daily practice, one that helps you lead your team beyond your title, as a person who genuinely wants to understand. With the business world evolving at a pace we've never seen before, *Inquisitive Leadership* and *Courageous Curiosity* will help you navigate change with more optimism, genuine excitement and effectiveness, and help others to do the same, not only unlocking your team's potential but your own .

Introducing The CAPPP Advantage™ Framework for Inquisitive Leadership

Summary: The CAPPP Advantage™ framework offers leaders a new approach to unlocking the potential of their teams to achieve better business results in a highly dynamic business environment. The five stages allow leaders to connect authentically with their teams, assess team members' capabilities with greater accuracy, tap into the value each team member brings to collective initiatives more effectively and connect each individual's "why" to the organization's purpose for improved engagement, creating an optimal environment for high-performance for individuals and the collective.

In my first functional leadership role, I led a team of managers who had been in their positions for some time. I'd been recently promoted, and several people in the group had applied for my job. Given the circumstances, I found myself steeped in their assumptions, resentments and, in some cases, intimidation tactics. Insecurity and fear have a funny way of manifesting themselves.

Despite the resistance I felt from the group and within myself, I knew there was a reason I was selected for the role: I love teaching and sharing my vision. Fortunately, I had inherited an amazing team of professionals who needed coaching and guidance to take their leadership to the next level, just as I did. So, I leaned into the curiosity that had guided me all my life. I got to know them as people, relating to them as individuals to build deeper connections instead of looking at them as the symbols I had in my mind.

I'm not "all business," so when we met for our one-on-ones, I used my sense of humor to find a common bond. I asked how long they had been with the team and what their likes and dislikes were, and I shared my questions ahead of our meeting so they had time to prepare. At the same time, I was always ready to respond to what was happening in the moment and to go "off script." It took a little time, but once we started to talk casually, we got to know each other. That gave me a chance to assess their values and form a picture of how they fit into the team, how they handled stress, what kind of thinkers they were and even if I had to be on guard because of any resentments they were harboring.

Once I overcame my hesitation and got out of my own way, I realized that my new position offered a fantastic opportunity to learn, grow, and get comfortable with being uncomfortable. Those casual conversations provided an open forum about our work together moving forward. It was not about communicating what I wanted from them, but rather about getting them to talk about themselves.

Did I always get it right? Absolutely not. But the more I learned about my team and got to know each individual, the more my fears, imposter syndrome and insecurities retreated, and the more the team members trusted me as their leader. That not only led to better performance, for myself and my team, but also genuine connection. I'm still in touch with two members of the team over 25 years later.

This early-career experience ultimately sparked the development of The CAPPP Advantage™ performance framework, though I didn't realize I was creating it at the time. It happened organically. Like most leaders in corporate America, I was frequently thrust into situations with no rule book. I knew that leading requires having faith when you can't see the outcome and trusting that you are making the right decisions with the information you have at that moment. However, I also realized that when leading in these situations, it was risky to, in essence, go without a framework. That's like driving onto the highway with so much rain pelting the windshield that you can't see a thing.

Unfortunately, I found that many executives felt forced to "drive" without a clear field of vision . Their companies were spending millions of dollars to solve a pressing challenge that had disrupted the organization's plans. However, they were devising new strategies and initiatives with very little clarity on the real problem at hand.

No one was asking the questions that would guide them to the information they needed to diagnose the situation and find the ideal path forward. Complicating this, these leaders rarely addressed the human side of situations, including unspoken beliefs, assumptions, and attitudes. However, interpersonal dynamics often influenced their business outcomes more than factors such as the business environment or a new competitor.

It soon became clear how I could help them. I developed an approach based on leading from a place of curiosity. The foundation of the approach is seeking new information. The more you learn from your team, the higher the quality of your decisions will be. As the team becomes more comfortable contributing, more individuals will share their ideas, and trust will build. This trust is needed to sustain high performance through the ebbs and flows of business.

In several decades of working with executives, The CAPPP Advantage™ methodology has helped leaders quickly identify situations in which it is essential to gather information early, ask questions that tap into their team's collective knowledge, and reach clarity on how to proceed before drawing a conclusion. The CAPPP Advantage™ empowers leaders with the tools to enter any business environment, conference room, or one-on-one setting and gather the necessary information to make better decisions. It allows them to move forward with confidence while building greater harmony on the team along the way.

Inquisitive Leadership is built around the mindset of *Courageous Curiosity*. The foundation of *Courageous Curiosity* is developing the skills to ask questions about whatever you don't understand in each business situation, including matters you are not comfortable with—and listening to the answers before forming an opinion or devising a strategy.

Inquisitive Leadership works. I know because I use it daily. As a leader at a major telecom company, I used the methods I now teach to build and lead high-performing teams that consistently exceeded our business unit's key performance indicators, even when the teams initially showed mediocre performance. Leading from a place of curiosity has also allowed me to build amazing relationships, not only as a leader but also as a business owner, coach, and thought leader. I have seen many of the leaders I coach apply the same ideas with similar success. In the pages to come, you'll learn through the case studies how leaders from very different backgrounds and experiences applied The CAPPP Advantage™ performance framework.

The five stages of Inquisitive Leadership

Practicing *Inquisitive Leadership* means adopting five-stages: Building Connection and Rapport, Assessing the Team, Valuing People, Understanding Purpose, and Cultivating Performance what I refer to as The CAPPP Advantage™ performance framework. This framework likely differs from others you have used because it helps leaders prioritize building relationships and understanding before delving into individuals' capabilities and organizational direction. Most companies, in my experience, do things the other way around.

The CAPPP Advantage™ Performance Model

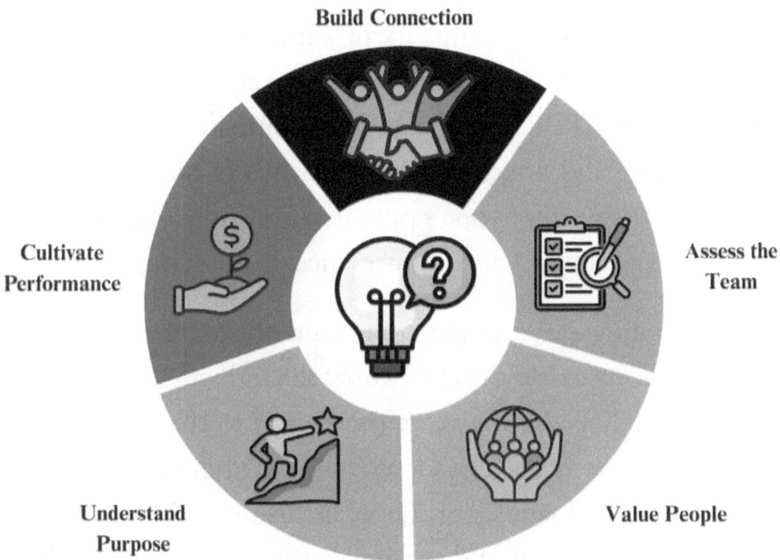

The CAPPP Advantage™ Performance Model, the foundational framework developed by Frederica A. Peterson

So, let's look at each stage:

1. Building Connection and Rapport: *Inquisitive Leadership* begins with fostering genuine relationships and camaraderie within your team. It is about understanding the existing dynamics and relationships within the group, as well as the individual team members' relationship to their work. Here is where you begin to understand the heartbeat of each team member. Who are they beyond their title and position? Where are there similarities and differences, and how do they fit into your overall relationship dynamic? Through genuine connection, you set the stage for open communication and building trust, both of which are essential to *Inquisitive Leadership.*

2. Assessing the Team: Once a leader has established trust and open lines of communication, they can effectively evaluate the team's strengths, skills, abilities, and capabilities, identifying the untapped potential that exists within the team. The quality of a leader's relationships with team members will directly impact the depth and accuracy of the assessment. Through The CAPPP Advantage™ performance framework, leaders learn to observe and assess their team members more accurately. They learn how to uncover everyone's potential over time and how to cultivate it for greater team impact and performance.

3. Valuing People: After assessing the team, the focus shifts to the people. Leaders do a deeper dive to get to know the individuals within the team, exploring who they are, the value they bring to the company and their contributions to its work. The focus is on identifying any barriers (mental health, psychological safety, or issues of inclusion/exclusion) that might be hindering their potential and recognizing how their unique differences, such as preferences, ways of working, and diversity (age, race, experience, education, gender, etc.), fuel the team's innovation and performance. This step is informed by both the initial connection and the subsequent assessment.

4. Understanding Purpose: Informed by a strong understanding of the people on a team and their potential, leaders can move onto Understanding Purpose. Developing this knowledge involves exploring the collective "why" of the team, as well as the work each person does. This includes understanding the impact of their work and how it fits into the larger organizational goals and metrics. It also encourages individuals to reflect on and actively share their personal motivations and goals with the leader. In this stage, every member of the team, including the leader, delves into their own collective "why," connecting it to the team's goals. This shared understanding of purpose is grounded in the reality of the team's collective identity and potential, providing direction and motivation. With many of the groups I work with, structured activities are a quick and highly effective way to unlock a team's shared purpose.

5. Cultivating Performance: The culmination of all the stages, Cultivating Performance, is built around a narrative that emphasizes that high achievement doesn't take place in a vacuum. It is the direct result of the environment the leader creates through the previous four stages: establishing a connection with the team, accurately assessing the capabilities of both the team and the individuals on it, understanding and valuing the people on the team, and aligning everyone around a shared purpose.

Cultivating high performance is like nurturing a garden. To produce a beautiful, vibrant garden, three things must be present:

1. You must genuinely care for the plants you are tending. That means understanding their unique needs for sun, soil, fertilizer, and even companionship. Every plant is different and reacts differently to environmental factors.

2. You must pay attention to how they are adapting to the environment and what they contribute to it. What makes them thrive? How do they add to the beauty of the landscape you are creating? Some thrive in pots, some like to be planted in the ground, and others love to wrap themselves around trestles.

Like a gardener, the leader must do the work to discover the unique strengths and weaknesses of each plant. For instance, I love roses. I was always under the assumption they had to be planted in the ground, but as I recently discovered, tea roses can live for years in pots. Who knew?

Then the leader must consider each plant they have selected for the garden. Is there anything in the environment that might hinder their growth or development? I've noticed that during the considerably hot summers in my area, I must be more mindful of my watering patterns, as well as the shade the plant is getting. If a plant is not producing blooms, I must evaluate its environment. Does it need more nutrients to grow? Are there any bugs that have gotten into the soil or leaves that I might need to eradicate? Maybe deer are munching away at my poor babies at night. All that to say, I must evaluate their environment to make sure nothing is getting in the way of their full potential.

3. *You need to understand why each plant was chosen for the garden.* Was it part of the overall landscape strategy, or a variety inherited with a new home?

Ultimately, every garden has a purpose, just as a team does. Maybe that purpose is to provide shade, bring the nourishment of fresh vegetables or herbs or create a welcoming environment on the property. Once we have connected with that purpose, the result is a beautiful garden. The same holds in the workplace, where we are cultivating a culture where every individual can thrive.

Inquisitive Leadership helps leaders develop both authentic relationships and understand how to be an effective leader through *Courageous Curiosity*. The leader plays a crucial role in establishing the foundation. Following the five stages of The CAPPP Advantage™ framework ensures that leaders can understand each team member and harness their full capabilities and contributions, helping the larger organization accelerate progress toward its most important goals.

In the next chapter, we'll get started with the first stage: Building Connection and Rapport. Once you master that concept, you'll be well prepared to move through the framework.

Key takeaways:

- *Inquisitive Leadership* is a new approach that ensures leaders can harness the full potential of their team through *Courageous Curiosity* by:

    * Connecting authentically

    * Assessing team members' capabilities with greater accuracy

    * Identifying the value each team member brings to collective initiatives more effectively

    * Connecting each individual's "why" to the organization's purpose

    * Leveraging the previous four stages to improve engagement and create an optimal environment for every individual on the team to thrive

- Every team has a purpose, and through *Courageous Curiosity* leaders have tremendous power to create environments where teams can thrive.

CHAPTER 2

Building Connection and Rapport

Summary: Authentic connection is the foundation of leadership. Connection allows leaders to build strong relationships in which trust and transparency foster the psychological safety needed to achieve team goals. Learning how to build connection with team members is the first and most essential step of The CAPPP Advantage™ framework. Building connection requires an ongoing conscious commitment, empathy, listening for clarity, and communication. Leaders often need to overcome unconscious bias, as well. Ultimately, connection allows leaders to increase engagement, innovation, and high performance.

A trainer on my team asked if she could speak with me privately during one of our company's events. She was someone who rarely came to me with problems, so I made time in between activities, even though my schedule was nearly full. At that time, our growth was so rapid that it was almost mind-numbing. All departments were running at full capacity. I started with 25 people in my organization, and it had grown to a little over 300 in just three years. Even with the new hires, we were managing an incredible workload that just kept expanding.

To meet the demands of the new-hire training that was essential to a culture where people were viewed as "only as good as your last project," my team had to run back-to-back classes with no breaks in between for three or four weeks straight. It was a punishing pace, but in a "figure it out, or move on" environment, it was necessary. There was no one to turn to for advice, unless you were among a select group mentored by our executive team. For those of us outside those circles, perhaps because we were from different backgrounds and ways of thinking, this was intimidating.

During that period, I often imagined that my team saw me as out of touch and overly demanding. Although I told them I appreciated all they were doing and shared my own feelings of vulnerability if mistakes took place in the chaos, I often left work feeling defeated. We completed the classes in record time, exceeded our KPIs, and racked up awards. However, our stress levels were high, and the topic of maintaining morale dominated our leadership meetings.

That was the atmosphere when the trainer came to me. I braced myself to hear about whatever new problem was at hand. "I just wanted to say how much we have all admired you for your transparency," she said. "Leaders in our organization always come across as perfect and polished, but you're someone we can really relate to and learn from. You're authentic, and I just want to let you know how much we appreciate you."

I was so stunned that I still don't remember how I responded. However, that moment of genuine, human-to-human connection shifted my perspective on myself as a leader and still resonates with me. It marked a profound transformation: I stopped viewing myself as someone everyone saw as a screw up or disliked and re-envisioned myself as a leader whom my team appreciated and wanted to emulate. That brief exchange taught me that connection, not control, is what gives us our ability to lead.

Connection as a leadership principle

This experience is a powerful reminder of why The CAPPP Advantage™ framework begins with connection. As leaders, we are part of a team. The trainer who approached me was three layers below me in the hierarchy, but she understood that a team isn't just the people who do the work; it is everyone involved in the group's performance. Everyone has a role to play and a job to do. Inquisitive Leaders understand that it takes mutual vulnerability, consistent effort on both sides, and time to weave connection into a team's fabric.

Each small, intentional action we take as leaders builds trust and helps individuals and teams thrive. Nurturing the right environment can support connection and the benefits it brings. An atmosphere of respect and empowerment encourages team members to contribute their unique skills, experiences, perspectives, and talents, leading to team cohesion.

In this chapter, we will explore how you can build connections as an Inquisitive Leader. I'll draw on what I learned leading fast-growing teams and in guiding many other leaders in the corporate world. A growing body of research in neuroscience and organizational psychology supports what I found to be true in my own career. I've included an overview of the research in Appendix I.

The neuroscience of trust and social bonding

Strong relationships between leaders and their team members are not just "nice to haves." They are a strategic advantage backed by science. Neuroscientific research sheds light on the biological mechanisms underlying trust and connection. Research consistently reflects their value.

Let's take a look at what is happening when trust and connection grow.

- **Our brain releases oxytocin:** Often referred to as the "bonding hormone," oxytocin starts flowing from our brains during positive social interactions.[1] Studies indicate that high-trust environments and positive leader-member interactions foster this flow, which, in turn, promotes prosocial behaviors, cooperation, and a willingness to take risks with others.

- **Key regions of our brains are activated:** The prefrontal cortex, amygdala, and striatum help us assess trustworthiness, understand social rewards, and regulate emotions. In an environment built on connection, these parts of our brain help us to establish mutual trust.

- **Our stress levels decline:** A high-trust environment lowers our stress levels, moving us from survival mode to thriving. This leads to improved focus, enhanced problem-solving, and better overall performance.

As you can see, many of these reactions happen automatically. The body responds to what it detects physically and emotionally, not necessarily to what leaders or coworkers say. When you create an environment of genuine connection, your team members will react on a biological level. That will influence how they feel, think, and behave, individually and as members of your larger group.[2]

How connection contributes to psychological safety

As Amy Edmondson, a professor of leadership at Harvard Business School, has pointed out, the most powerful drivers of team success are trust and psychological safety.[3] In a landmark study in 1999, she demonstrated that teams with high psychological safety— meaning those in which the members don't think they will be punished or humiliated for speaking up with ideas, questions, concerns or mistakes—are significantly more innovative and effective. When team members feel genuinely connected to you as their leader, they perceive you as approachable and supportive. Individuals on your team will feel more comfortable being their authentic selves and contributing fully when there is psychological safety. That comfort level can, in turn, lead to improved performance for your team.

A high-trust, psychologically safe environment rarely emerges by accident; it is cultivated through leaders who take the time to build genuine, trusting relationships. It might seem obvious that people will communicate more openly and perform better if they trust that you've "got their back," but leaders are not always aware of what it takes to create psychological safety or the signs that team members do not feel it. We may unintentionally create an unsafe environment. My motto is, "No one gets up in the morning wanting to offend anyone." In this chapter, you'll learn what you can do to create a more trusting, psychologically safe environment for your team. Whether psychological safety exists or not isn't entirely in your control. It depends on each team member's experiences, both past and present. Just because you may not experience what they do, does not mean it is not happening. It is important to pay close attention to what you are hearing from your employees when the topic turns to feeling unsafe. Feeling unsafe can show up as discomfort being vulnerable by sharing ideas, not feeling valued as a member of the team, being excluded from conversations, etc.

This is when *Inquisitive Leadership* can guide you, helping you to tap into your *Courageous Curiosity* and ask them the right questions: What are they feeling? What is causing it? The information you gathered from previous observations and assessments, if you have done any, can help, providing context and a starting point for a conversation built on understanding.

Some of what team members share when you ask questions may have nothing to do with what you can see firsthand. While you have no control over the past, you can still actively try to understand someone's experience and the influences that may be contributing. As you seek a path forward, it is essential to validate what is important to each individual by listening to them from their perspective and not your own and to avoid discrediting or devaluing their experiences. Sometimes people simply need to feel seen and heard, and to know that you are truly listening to them.

When a workplace culture values differences and inclusion, it is easier to build the trust that helps a team thrive. That is especially true when you are moving at warp speed, and it is easy to make mistakes. How will you handle something that goes wrong? Will it be addressed behind closed or open doors? How you address mishaps matters significantly to your team and can help you avoid communication mistakes that cost you their trust. As Amy Edmondson's work shows, psychological safety supports better learning outcomes: Team members who experience psychological safety are more willing to admit errors and learn from them.[3] In a psychologically safe environment, they are also more willing to air diverse perspectives and discuss them openly to find solutions. As a leader, this will take a tremendous weight off your shoulders. You don't have to have all the answers if you have set the stage for your team to come to you with them.

The "how" of building connection

Let's return to the story I shared at the opening of this chapter. The reason the trainer felt comfortable approaching me to ask for a few minutes together was a practice I established from the moment I started my job. Understanding that connecting with *every* member of the team would help me perform better, I included coordinators and assistants on my meeting roster. I met with my direct reports weekly, their direct reports monthly, supervisors on the team quarterly, and everyone else for yearly one-on-ones. Additionally, we held all-hands managers' meetings twice a year and full department summits once a year over several days.

The result was a genuine connection. I didn't just know team members, like the trainer, as names on an org chart—I saw them as individuals. They had families, aspirations, successes, and failures; they were people with unique talents, gifts, and abilities. And I did my best to appreciate and value all of it, learning about them and myself as we got to know each other.

While some leaders might think all the time I put into relationship-building wasn't necessary, I knew it would ultimately fuel our growth and improve the bottom line. Regular communication fostered a collaborative mindset and approach, enabling us to work together successfully as a high-performing team. Our team's loyalty and work ethic made us a force to be reckoned with.

The results told the story: Over three years, I expanded the team from five small regional teams to five large, multifunctional regional ones. We consistently ranked as the number one region among our peers for many years. How did we do it? Connection. With everyone working in unison, achieving exceptional results became the norm.

Nine ways to build strong relationships on your team

The foundation of meaningful relationships are trust and respect, rather than being everyone's best friend. Here are some ways you can intentionally foster the connections that support these relationships, with real-world examples and reflection prompts to help you put each step into practice:

1. Be present and accessible

Example: A senior leader at a mid-sized tech firm blocked 30 minutes weekly to walk the floor, greet employees, and ask what they were working on. The simple gesture led to more spontaneous problem-solving conversations.

- **Why it matters:** Presence signals value. People feel respected when leaders make time for them.

- **How to do it:** Schedule regular one-on-one check-ins beyond task updates. Show up—physically or virtually—for moments that matter.

- **Reflect:** How often do you make yourself truly available to your team? What one small change could you make this week to increase your presence?

2. Practice active listening

Example: A manager noticed her team was disengaged in meetings. She started each session by asking, "What's on your mind today?" and listened without interrupting. Within weeks, participation and idea sharing improved dramatically.

- **Why it matters:** Employees want to feel heard, not managed.

- **How to do it:** Focus fully when someone is speaking. Paraphrase what you hear. Avoid rushing to solutions.

- **Reflect:** When was the last time a team member felt truly heard by you? How do you know?

3. Show genuine interest in individuals

Example: An Inquisitive Leader in a healthcare setting began asking nurses about their long-term goals during quarterly check-ins. One nurse expressed an interest in leadership, and within a year, she was mentored into a supervisory role.

- **Why it matters:** Understanding your team's aspirations helps align opportunities with their growth.

- **How to do it:** Learn what energizes or drains your team members, and use that insight to tailor support.

- **Reflect:** How well do you know each person's career aspirations on your team? Whose goals are still a mystery to you?

4. Build trust through consistency

Example: After a failed product launch, a director admitted his role in the oversight during an all-hands meeting. His willingness to own mistakes set the tone for a culture of accountability.

- **Why it matters:** Trust is built through reliable, repeated actions—not one-time gestures.

- **How to do it:** Communicate openly, follow through on promises, and admit when you don't have all the answers.

- **Reflect:** Do your actions consistently match your words? Where could you increase transparency or follow-through?

5. Recognize and appreciate contributions

Example: A team leader in a remote environment started a "Friday shout-out" email where team members could highlight one another's wins. Morale and cross-team collaboration increased noticeably.

- **Why it matters:** Recognition reinforces connection and desired behaviors.

- **How to do it:** Be specific about the contributions you value—both privately and publicly.

- **Reflect:** Who on your team deserves recognition this week, and how will you express it?

6. Invite and act on feedback

Example: A vice president regularly asked her team, "What's one thing I can start or stop doing to better support you?" When she acted on feedback to improve meeting structures, team productivity spiked.

- **Why it matters:** Building relationships is a two-way process. Asking for feedback is a way to model openness.

- **How to do it:** Regularly ask for input—and implement what you can.

- **Reflect:** When was the last time you asked your team for feedback about your leadership? What did you do with their input?

7. Support development and growth

Example: A manufacturing supervisor identified an employee with strong analytical skills and encouraged them to take on a data project outside their usual role. This not only developed new skills but boosted the individual's loyalty to the team.

- **Why it matters:** Relationships deepen when employees see leaders invested in their future.

- **How to do it:** Offer mentorship, learning opportunities, and stretch assignments.

- **Reflect:** Who on your team is ready for their next challenge, and how can you help them step into it?

8. Create a culture of psychological safety

Example: A project manager made it a rule to share one personal learning from each project phase, framing mistakes as steppingstones. Team members began volunteering their own missteps, leading to faster improvements.

- **Why it matters:** Without psychological safety, relationships remain surface-level.

- **How to do it:** Normalize learning from mistakes, encourage questions, and protect people when they take thoughtful risks.

- **Reflect:** What have you done recently to signal that it's safe to take risks or admit mistakes on your team?

Key characteristics of Inquisitive Leaders who practice connection

Every Inquisitive Leader must master two key pillars of communication: Empathy and listening for clarity. Let's look at why they are important.

1. **Empathy:** This means seeking to understand the experiences and emotions of others to foster greater connection. Inquisitive Leaders use inquiry to build relationships, not just gather information. They ask questions that show care and concern, not just curiosity.

   Asking the right questions can help. Here are some sample questions:

   * "Could you walk me through what happened from your point of view?"

   * "What does an optimal outcome of this situation look like for you?"

   * "How can I help you feel more supported?"

2. **Listening for clarity:** Inquisitive Leaders ask questions that will help them prioritize their own activities and those of the team, seeking the

"one thing" that is likely to have the most significant impact. They create space for other perspectives, listen to learn (not to respond), and ask the team questions to define success clearly. They mitigate ambiguity by using Courageous Curiosity instead of authority.

Here are some sample questions:

* "How would you define success?"

* "What actions would have the greatest impact right now?"

* "Based on what you know, how would you proceed?"

Barriers to connection

Inquisitive Leaders also recognize that many obstacles can block communication and ultimately connection. It is easy for biases, preferences, and habits to overshadow your quest to connect with others. Our own unquestioned thinking can block communication with others who are different from us.

Let's explore some of the most significant roadblocks to connection with others.

Unconscious sabotage. Teams with more diversity are far more innovative, productive, and profitable than those that are more homogeneous. Much as we know this, it is easiest to form connections with people we like, who are familiar to us, or who share some similarities with us. As an Inquisitive Leader, it is essential to understand the factors that could prevent you from connecting with your team or with individuals on it. Unconscious bias is a very real part of the discussion.

The biggest differences we have as human beings are often hidden under the surface. They can show up in many ways beyond race, gender, or disability. In my experience, the most significant area of difference within teams is neurodiversity: how we think, learn, do our work, and process information. Sometimes, neurodiversity is obvious, but not always.

It is human nature to react to what we see. The meaning we assign to differences flows from deep in our subconscious . This meaning is subjective. It is shaped by our lived and learned experiences, from our formative years until the present. The meaning we take away catalyzes our reactions to life experiences, people, and environments.

What we see is just the packaging; it's what's inside us–our communication style, temperament, tendencies, and preferences–that cause us to react. We often associate these automatic behaviors with physical identifiers. One example is responding to someone in a "knee-jerk" way because of their difference from us or their diversity. This is a bias that can prevent us from connecting with someone.

Leaders who understand the value of *Courageous Curiosity* learn how to manage these reactions differently and how to transcend differences to connect with every member of their team, thereby building stronger connections within the team.

How "connected" leaders can manage conflict

No matter how much connection you build with your team, managing conflict will still be part of your job as a leader. More than 50% of the leaders I coach are actively working to resolve a dispute or difficult employee situation.

I recently coached a client, Michelle, who had been hired from outside of her company to lead a team of marketing professionals as director. One person on the team, Cheryl, had been performing many of the responsibilities of this role for four years and had applied for the newly created position. From the time Michelle started her job, Cheryl had been difficult, challenging Michelle's decisions, berating other employees, and openly displaying undermining behaviors that were hurting the team's morale, not to mention ruffling the feathers of some of the senior leaders. However, the senior leaders had not given her much feedback, as no one wanted to deal with her usual antics.

Michelle was losing patience. She had empathized with Cheryl's frustrations about being passed over for the position, but after 10 months in it, she recognized, correctly, that the empathy needed to stop and the work needed to begin.

I shared a perspective with her that has helped many of my clients in similar situations. First, I asked if she ever set clear expectations with Cheryl about what her role requires.

Her answer, not surprisingly, was "No," the typical response I get.

"Why not?" I asked her.

Michelle did not have an answer to that question. It was not something she had considered.

The first rule of leading others is that people will live up to the expectations you have set for them. When you don't establish an expectation, then you are leaving it up to someone else to set it for you. If you are in conflict, their expectation is misaligned with yours. It's on you to set expectations and be clear about boundaries to prevent and resolve conflicts. (Bonus thought: That goes for your personal life, too!)

Michelle understood that she needed to establish expectations for Cheryl and gain agreement. Then she needed to hold Cheryl accountable to that agreement.

She asked me how she would do that. You may have that question, too. Consider what the foundation of being an Inquisitive Leader is: *Courageous Curiosity*. Before setting expectations, she needed to start by asking questions that would help her understand the situation at hand with Cheryl and the reasons Cheryl was acting as she did. Only then could she respond effectively as a leader.

Keep in mind that the purpose of holding someone accountable is not simply calling them out on something; it's ultimately about ensuring they take responsibility for their actions. In keeping with this mindset as an Inquisitive Leader, always lead with the question, "Why?" Why did someone act that way? Why were they comfortable with that behavior? What did they believe the outcome would be from that action? What would be another way of looking at that situation? That will help you determine what to do next.

For instance, in a recent meeting, Cheryl had made a decision for the entire team without consulting with Michelle first. One of Michelle's partners and all the company's leaders were present. Her first step as an Inquisitive Leader was to ask Cheryl what made her feel comfortable making that decision without consulting with her first. Michelle might easily have assumed that Cheryl was being blatantly disrespectful. Instead, she chose to ask a question. Granted, the disrespect might have been present, but Michelle still needed to ask some clarifying questions to get to the root of the issue and take the appropriate actions.

I have seen it too many times: acting based on assumptions alone is like walking on a tightrope. At any moment, you could take a wrong step, and that could lead to a setback in your relationship with your employee that is extremely difficult to overcome. Cheryl may have felt comfortable making that decision because she had been in that position for years before Michelle ever joined the company. Now, that is a different perspective. This possibility is why Courageous Curiosity holds so much power.

When Michelle asked Cheryl about her behavior, she found out that Cheryl was frustrated because she believed she was more qualified for the role than Michelle. Cheryl did not see how her behavior was impacting her own image or the career aspirations of others on the team. Michelle is now actively working with Cheryl to identify her next step, because she is having a difficult time continuing to work under Michelle. Although Michelle inherited a difficult, conflict-laden situation, the best resolution was to establish mutual respect and set expectations for effective communication, which she achieved.

With this story in mind, the next time you need to confront a difficult employee situation, consider asking yourself, "Did I set an expectation?" If so, then you need to understand why the employee failed to meet it. If their behavior clearly does not line up, give them the benefit of the doubt initially. Next, realize the impact of their behavior may not be as evident to them as you suppose. Then start asking them questions, so you understand where they are coming from. "Why did you...?" or "What was your intention...?" "How do you think that impacted...?" After you have gained some insight, provide them with clarity on the impact of their actions on your relationship with them or their relationship with the team, and ask for their thoughts.

What's key is asking questions that help them to realize the impact of their behavior. Simply correcting or reprimanding them for their actions does not have the same effect. Thinking and talking it through naturally holds them accountable. Having them voice their inappropriate behavior will force them to own it.

To bring the conversation to a close, ask, "Is there anything you would do differently next time?" Let's be clear: when you do this the first few times, the team member may try to put the onus of asking the question back on you. For instance, they might ask, "What do you think I should do differently?" Instead of providing an answer, ask them to answer their own question and explain your reasoning, such as "It is important for me to understand what you think you should do." Remember, your response should always be a question. You want to understand, not defend someone's behavior. You are simultaneously being clear and setting a boundary. If they mention any changes they would make, and these align with what you would like them to do, ask if there is any support they need from you to be successful with the behavior change. If the changes they suggest would not be helpful, you will need a more extended discussion, so they understand what is required of them.

In some cases, it will become clear that someone has a different agenda from doing the best job possible. They may have a hostile intent and no intention to change. Someone with their own agenda might say there is nothing they would change in their behavior. At that point, one helpful question to ask is, "What would be the risk in *not* changing your behavior?"

Typically, the risk is not meeting expectations at work or losing their jobs, outcomes they may not have considered. In these cases, it is best to set expectations and then start moving to a performance plan. I highly recommend engaging with your HR partner to ensure that you, the employee, and the company are protected. That is what you have an HR team for.

It is out of your control if someone doesn't have the team's best interests in mind and is unwilling to change or claims to want to change their behavior but is not taking the steps to which they've agreed. In those cases, you may need to talk with them about looking for employment elsewhere. However, if they are open to changing their behavior, follow that up by asking if there is anything you can do to support them as they navigate the behavior change.

The Inquisitive Leader's conflict resolution formula

Conflicts tend to crop up when you least expect them. Just as martial artists practice moves, like breaking a wrist grab, until they become automatic, leaders need to have a few strategies that they can rely on under any circumstances. Any time you must resolve a conflict, it's helpful to have the Inquisitive Leader's conflict resolution formula in your back pocket—and depend on it:

Set expectations. Right out of the gate, make sure your expectations align with the team member's understanding. Remember, everyone had a journey before your paths met. Those experiences shaped their paradigms of the world, which fuel the decisions they make. What is evident to you is not always apparent to someone else.

Hold them accountable. Ask questions to gain clarity on the behavior. Instead of calling someone out on the bad behavior, have a conversation about what happened. What impact do they think it had? If what they say doesn't line up with the facts, help bring clarity to the problem and the effects of their actions.

Practice. If you have not been implementing these leadership tactics, they may require some practice. But they will eventually become natural—and you and your team will be on the path to cultivating high performance.

Addressing and resolving conflict doesn't have to be a heavy lift. It only becomes so when you are doing all the work. Use *Courageous Curiosity* and the art of inquiry to understand the role you play, as the leader, as well as the roles played by the team members involved in a conflict. This is paramount for their development and for building trust with you. Ultimately will allow you to tap the potential of all your team members.

Key takeaways:

- Nurturing a good environment can support connection and build stronger relationships with your team.

- The body responds to what it detects physically and emotionally, not necessarily to what leaders or coworkers say.

- The most powerful drivers of team success are trust and psychological safety.

- Psychologically safe environments are created and cultivated by leaders who take the time to build genuine, trusting relationships.

- No one gets up in the morning wanting to offend.

- Managing conflict is an important part of your job as a leader. Asking the right questions and setting expectations can help you manage conflict successfully.

CHAPTER 3

Assessing Your Team

Summary: Accurately assessing team members' capabilities and contributions is a foundation of Inquisitive Leadership. Within The CAPPP Advantage™ framework, assessment goes beyond the measurement of someone's skills. It is about using strategic inquiry to understand what motivates the individuals on the team, what barriers they face, and what potential lies dormant within them. To assess team members with accuracy and open the door to opportunities for growth, Inquisitive Leaders must examine their own biases and assumptions.

When I started a six-month coaching engagement with a young executive who was being groomed for promotion, we had a tough time with chemistry. I found him to be highly judgmental, often very rude, and not very supportive of his staff.

At his core, he was a very smart and ambitious leader. Though he had only been in his role for a few years, he was already getting noticed by higher-ups and seemed destined to reach the C-suite. However, he struggled to lead his team because he behaved as if everything was about him. He constantly compared himself to his peers, thinking he was significantly better than they were. He focused on what he needed and how he wanted things, not what would benefit individual employees or the team. He was not self-aware enough to realize how his actions were affecting his team and could not figure out why he had not been promoted yet.

It required a lot of patience to observe his behavior in our group sessions. As a coach, I made a conscious effort to stay out of the judgment zone. However, this guy needed a reality check. After an interaction with one of his colleagues had gone poorly, he set up a time to meet with me to discuss the interaction. His colleague had shared some hard truths with him that were difficult for him to process.

Whatever his colleague said to him hit home, and he now saw himself in a much different light. What I experienced in that session was a version of the executive I had not seen in any of our other sessions. The interaction had humbled him, and he was seeking understanding as we discussed his relationship with work. I asked him some tough questions to get to the root of the motivations for his ambitions. We could both see that work was defining him, and the more he accomplished, the more positively he saw himself. His self-worth was completely tied up in it. It was our most productive session.

After that meeting, our subsequent ones went very well. I had written him off as a self-absorbed, selfish leader who was doing more damage than good and couldn't see his possibilities before that. But I came to realize he was actually likable but just misguided and immature. After our subsequent sessions, he became more self-aware, more thoughtful in his interactions, and open to feedback. He was more comfortable being vulnerable, which helped him form a stronger bond with the program participants.

Why assessment matters

The coaching experience I just shared underscored the importance of assessing team members accurately. Assessment, in The CAPPP Advantage™

framework, refers to evaluating someone's skills, capabilities, and potential, considering both "hard," measurable elements of their repertoire and "soft" skills, such as empathy and the ability to "read the room."

Because the young executive initially rubbed me the wrong way, I almost gave up on helping him. It was only after I stepped back and assessed him through the lens of *Inquisitive Leadership* that I could see his capabilities and help him unlock his potential.

What if I had written him off after the first session? He may have chalked it up to being too good for coaching and never tapped into his potential to become a better leader. I also would have lost the opportunity to improve my own abilities as a leader and coach. The experience served as a valuable reminder for me of a key point we discussed in Chapter 2: to connect, we need to overcome our biases. We all have biases and narratives; admitting this is the challenge.

I have confronted this in myself: I tend to gravitate toward people who are relational, witty, and quick on their feet. Throughout many years of leadership development work, I have given considerable weight to these characteristics when evaluating leaders. The narrative I have created for myself is that people who embody these traits will perform best.

However, in a business environment where teams are leaner than in the past, every person on a team, including those you don't "click" with, has the power to make positive and significant contributions. As leaders, we need to lean on all our people to deliver exceptional results. There might be brilliance behind the qualities that rub us the wrong way, as in the case of the executive I coached. Our challenge as leaders is learning how to transcend behaviors that trigger us personally, so we can guide our teams much more effectively.

Assessment is a powerful tool to help you break out of unseen thinking patterns that may be holding you back from viewing team members through the lens of "what is possible" or their potential. To unleash their talents and abilities, you must first understand the narrative you have created about your ideal team members, then recognize and break out of any limiting scripts playing in your head. With that foundation in place, you will be ready to assess talent with a fully open mind.

"Unmasking" your team

To embark successfully on the assessment process, it is essential to understand masks—public faces that don't fully reflect who we are. Many people put on masks in the workplace, showing you what they think you want to see. The reason is simple: to hide. They fear that others will not accept them in their full authenticity. Their past experiences have shown them that they will be rejected, so they adopt a "safe" professional mask that makes everyone comfortable and allows them to keep their jobs.

As a leader, you might be asking, "What is wrong with maintaining a professional demeanor and fitting into the corporate culture?" The problem is that a mask is a false representation of oneself. Individuals and teams only perform at their best when people feel free to be their authentic selves. When people feel they must wear masks, your culture and individual team members' performance suffer, ultimately limiting the team's potential.

Beyond this, as a leader, a big part of your job is casting. It's up to you to assign the right people to the right roles, initiatives, and projects, almost like a movie director. When you judge someone based solely on their surface-level qualities, you may not be aware of their full capabilities and could miss out on what they might contribute to the team and the company. You could also unwittingly contribute to churn on your team. At a time when many companies struggle with attracting and retaining the best talent, you are an important gatekeeper to opportunity within the company. Team members who don't think they will be able to express their talents fully will become disengaged or leave.

Keep in mind that within the larger corporate culture, there is also a team culture, and you are responsible for co-creating that. Individuals on the team will look to you for signals on how you expect them to perform and behave. Assessing every member of your team fairly and accurately will let them know that it is worthwhile to reveal the capabilities that may be hidden behind their masks. By learning how to assess their capabilities—and acting on what you discover—you will enhance the team's performance and your own.

Adopting the Inquisitive Leadership mindset in your assessments

A traditional leader lets someone's performance speak for itself. An Inquisitive Leader recognizes that a corporate environment may be more comfortable for some team members than others. This approach prioritizes getting to know each individual on a deeper level to understand their true potential.

Assessment, in the world of *Inquisitive Leadership*, involves evaluating someone's "objective" strengths and weaknesses and how they work with the team through formal measures (personality tests), and listening to their ideas, experiences, struggles, and what is in their hearts. This allows you, as a leader, to create new narratives about each individual and their potential and to make more informed, inclusive decisions about which opportunities to make available to them.

Inquisitive Leadership isn't always a linear process. Tapping into your gut instincts or intuition, which resides at a deeper level of awareness, is part of assessment. While our inner knowing doesn't always follow a clear-cut path or provide a definitive blueprint for action, it serves as a guide through feelings or a sense that something isn't quite right or there is more to know.

In the case of the executive I coached, my intuition added to my more "objective" findings. I tend to get curious when people display protective or disruptive behaviors. It challenges me to deal with my own discomfort. Even more, I lean into the belief that humans want to be accepted, feel good about themselves, and be comfortable.

In the instance of this executive, I knew instinctively that the desire to see himself as better than everyone else came from somewhere. It could have been a protective mechanism that would deflect anyone from challenging him.

Creating/facilitating a safe environment where everyone feels accepted and valued deflates behaviors like this. A safe environment empowers the others on the team to make changes in their own behavior, which is what happened here. Sometimes assessing is more about stepping back and observing to figure out the correct approach, not jumping in to fix things. I must fight that urge myself, but when we trust the process, the assessment becomes not only organic but also accurate.

Some leaders shy away from looking under the surface out of fear that things might get too "personal." Inquisitive Leadership will help you to transcend any discomfort you feel, allowing you to learn more about the people who work for you while still maintaining appropriate professional boundaries. It will help you avoid making assumptions and assess what each individual can contribute to the team.

Asking the right questions

Inquisitive Leadership is built on asking the right questions to gain deeper insights and using what you learn to unlock the potential of individuals, teams, and organizations. Asking purpose-driven questions can help you make daily assessments of team members' mindsets and capabilities, and recalibrate them in real-time, keeping in mind that people evolve constantly.

In a mindset of *Courageous Curiosity*, you allow the other person to lead you to the answers you need. By embracing *Courageous Curiosity* and a systems mindset that considers the organization's needs at the same time, you can unlock powerful insights that will help team members grow and ultimately strengthen your performance as a group.

Asking questions with *Courageous Curiosity* means focusing on the *why* of someone's decisions. Imagine if you were asking about a route they took in a car. Why did they take that path? What experiences informed that decision? What should you expect if you take this route? Once you listen to someone's answers, you can evaluate if their responses align with their actions and respond accordingly.

When you allow a team member to lead you through their thinking, you are giving them the wheel to drive the car, and you are in the passenger seat. They are taking you on the journey, and you are taking notes along the way. The information they volunteer will allow you to make a more accurate assessment.

Two types of questions for Inquisitive Leaders to master. Asking both purpose-driven questions and systems- driven questions will help you to become a stronger leader. As you practice Inquisitive Leadership, you will develop a good sense of when each type of question is most useful.

1. **Purpose-driven questions:** Reflecting Courageous Curiosity, these questions will help you to understand the "why" behind someone's decisions, behaviors, and outcomes. Purpose-driven questions focus on root causes, not symptoms, and help you approach challenges with a learner-centric mindset, not just as a problem-solver.

   Sample questions:

   * "How does this line up with our overarching goals?"

   * "What else do we need to consider to achieve these results?"

   * "What has already been done to address the issue?

   * What did we discover?"

2. **System driven questions:** These inquiries encourage the cross-pollination of ideas, fostering a collaborative approach. They are designed to help you understand the relationships between people, processes, and outcomes. Driven by intellectual curiosity, these questions will help you understand how different parts of the organization or environment interact with one another. When there is a problem, these questions can, like purpose-driven questions, help you uncover patterns, not just symptoms, and use data-driven insights to identify and prevent recurring issues, as well as discover and capitalize on new opportunities. Here are some sample questions:

   * "If we looked at this through the lens of another department, what might they see that we don't?"

   * "What if we combine two ideas that don't normally go together and see what we get?"

   * "Who else will be affected by this change?"

Assessing team members without bias

Beyond asking the right questions, use formal assessment tools such as The CAPPP Advantage™, Everything DiSC®, The Five Behaviors®, EQI 2.0®, or StrengthsFinder®. These tools can help you see team members through new lenses. As you ask questions and conduct formal testing, do frequent reality checks. Are you taking your own biases into account? Are you recalibrating your overall assessment of each team member and their capabilities?

Sometimes, our biases can introduce incorrect meaning into what we observe when we ask questions or conduct formal assessments. It is essential to adopt a neutral perspective if someone approaches something differently from you, whether it is how they use their critical thinking skills, make decisions, execute tasks, or perceive situations. What you view as a "must" may be a preference. There could be several routes to achieving a desired result for the team, including some you may never have considered.

Keep in mind that we often move at the will of what psychoanalyst Sigmund Freud called our Id. He identified the Id as "an instinctual component of our personality," one motivated by urges to satisfy basic needs, urges, and desires. When we are led by the Id, deep in our unconscious, we can act according to basic drives or a wish to protect ourselves, literally or metaphorically, and in doing so, alienate individuals on the team. We need to be aware and mindful of the Id, so we don't evaluate people or choose favorites based on who serves our Id the most.

I saw firsthand how damaging this could be when I worked with a leader who was new to the company but had previously worked for another firm for over 25 years. He was having a tough time working with his new manager. In his previous high-ranking role, he oversaw a budget exceeding $1 million, managing multiple teams across an entire region, and supervising several layers of leadership. For the most part, he worked autonomously. In this new role, he worked for a micro-manager. Despite his decades of experience as a high-ranking and respected leader, his boss treated him as if he were a new supervisor. If the leader didn't perform a task the way the boss preferred to do it, then it was wrong. If the leader took notes in meetings, it was considered strange, and the leader was labeled as incompetent. It was a difficult thing to watch since I had been through something similar.

This leader was being unfairly assessed. The boss did not hesitate to express concerns about this employee and his lack of confidence in the new hire's ability to do the work. However, when other leaders worked with this same individual, they were impressed with his work and did not understand why their boss was not seeing what everyone else was. It is unfortunate, but this boss demonstrated unconscious bias, and in the end, it cost them a very talented employee. The new leader left after about a year.

I have seen this many times in the corporate world. By making the mistake of assessing what is unique about someone as a defect, rather than a gift, we can dim some of our brightest stars. By becoming aware of this possibility as we assess, we can prevent it and move on to the next stage in the Inquisitive Leadership process: Valuing People.

Key takeaways:

- Assessments are critical tools you can use with your team to be more effective in your role as a leader.

- Your ability to create an environment in which you can accurately assess talent, without bias, is a key to reducing attrition.

- Avoid jumping to conclusions without concrete evidence. Take time to sit back and simply observe.

- Every person on the team matters, even those you don't click with.

- You effectively assess the talent on your team to ensure you are leveraging their impact.

- Use intuition as a guide as you dig beneath the surface.

- Have an open mind; this will allow you to see different perspectives and new possibilities.

Valuing People

Summary: Most successes and failures in an organization have their origins in relationships between people. In Valuing People, leaders learn to deeply understand individual team members' capabilities, motivations, and barriers to performance. Inclusion, psychological safety, and mental health all come into play, and understanding how they interact is essential to supporting innovation and achieving team goals.

When I first started coaching Brian, a promising leader in a tech company, he was positioning himself for a promotion but felt very frustrated by his interactions with his supervisor, Kyra. They had very different professional styles: Brian was hands-on and highly collaborative with his team; Kyra was visionary, highly strategic, and direct, and from his point of view, detached and bad at making decisions. Kyra, for her part, doubted his readiness for a strategic role due to his tactical thinking and focus on details.

In my initial sessions with Brian, we did some work to help him better understand Kyra's behaviors and motivations. When conflicts arose, I encouraged him to consider alternative perspectives and to adapt his communication style to hers, focusing more on the bigger picture and less on what he considered minutiae.

Brian committed to working on his communication with Kyra when they had the opportunity to work closely together over several weeks. They were preparing for crucial senior leadership meetings with the board, vendor partners, and other key stakeholders, which involved collecting and analyzing data. As Brian got this exposure to Kyra's strategic work, he began to understand why she stayed focused on the company's vision and her own for their department. As he gained a deeper understanding of the business from her vantage point, he developed immense respect for Kyra's forward-thinking vision and ability to connect complex business elements. This new perspective allowed Brian to develop a better working relationship with Kyra and to contribute his expertise more credibly to senior leaders, elevating his own contributions. By being willing to rethink his initial views, Brian experienced remarkable growth and ultimately earned the promotion he was seeking. His growth now benefits his team, and he has helped team members see how their work aligns with the broader strategy and to operate more effectively together. He is now, in turn, challenging their perspectives.

Recently, Brian interviewed for a senior position. Though he didn't get the role, the feedback he received was overwhelmingly positive. He had left a lasting impression, establishing himself as a rising star within the organization. Everyone noted his significant growth, which they found commendable. His relationship with Kyra has completely transformed, leaving Brian more confident than ever about his future and their collaboration.

How understanding team dynamics can fuel peak performance

As Brian's story illustrates, almost all successes and failures in any organization come down to its people. Doing a deeper dive into the individuals within the team and exploring the value they bring to both your business unit and the company, as a whole, is one of the most important steps you can take to lead a team to peak performance. That is why Valuing People is the next stage in The CAPPP Advantage™ framework. Valuing People is the process of fully understanding and embracing the unique qualities of your team members. Once you understand people as individuals, you can identify all of their capabilities to help them reach their full potential.

As we discussed in Chapter 1, Valuing People starts with identifying any barriers (mental health, psychological safety, or issues of inclusion/exclusion) that might be hindering the potential of someone on the team, whether that individual is yourself or a colleague It also includes exploring how diversity in age, race, experience, education, gender, etc. fuels the innovation and performance of the team.

 The work you have done in the Building Connection and Rapport and Assess the Team stages of The CAPPP Advantage™ framework will inform your work in this stage. However, Valuing People is a less linear process than assessing your team. It will require you to lean into your intuitive nature and gut instincts. What are you sensing? What do you notice about how your team members interact with each other, and with you? When are they more excited and passionate about their work, and when aren't they? Do they take longer than average to do certain assignments? When they share ideas and feedback with you, what is being left unsaid? Do you find it difficult to communicate with them, or to understand the way they communicate or do their work? Oftentimes, our preferences can bias our ability to see the value in others. Asking questions like this will help you understand each team member's strengths, weaknesses, communication style, and approaches to work—and how they contribute to the overall dynamics of the team. The answers to the questions will provide you with the opportunity to build stronger relationships and foster more trust, ultimately bringing out the best in your team. Some of the benefits include greater morale and engagement, more effective delegation and problem-solving, increased productivity and performance, and a more positive work culture.[4]

As you are Valuing People, don't forget to turn your lens to someone you may have overlooked: yourself. It is important to understand your own strengths and weaknesses as a leader. This is where I highly recommend taking a 360 assessment to become more self-aware and better understand the impact of your behavior on yourself and others.

Prioritizing psychological safety

In Chapter 3, we discussed the importance of psychological safety. As you focus on Valuing People, you'll find that you will be more successful on many fronts if your team experiences psychological safety. Team members may not always be able to articulate that they lack psychological safety, so pay attention to how they interact in meetings. Is everyone speaking up? Are they supporting one another in their contributions, or is someone always getting more airtime? How are they talking to each other? How are they talking about each other? Is it with respect? Are you more comfortable with one person's communication style than another's? If so, how does this indirectly impact how the team interacts with them? Does the atmosphere in the meeting allow space for everyone to contribute? Are all ideas heard and acknowledged? Is the small talk before meetings inclusive of everyone in the room? These day-to-day things may seem small, but they make an environment safe for your entire team.

If you are reading about psychological safety because it is an area you need to improve on, be intentional. Bring everyone together and let them know this subject is important to you and that you want to know how they are feeling. In some environments, bringing the group together and discussing this will be a welcome step. For other teams, this may feel very intimidating. If your observations indicate that a few team members would benefit from a more private discussion to express their true feelings, consider that option. It is not just "on you" to create psychological safety. It takes the team to make this work. You just need to be emotionally in tune enough to catch the signals that someone isn't feeling safe and determine what, in the team dynamic, is undermining psychological safety.

Expectation and accountability support psychological safety. When you tolerate something as the leader, the team will tolerate it. You are the compass.

Think of the things leaders will let pass or won't accept. There are outcomes from what we tolerate. If you see something, say something. Voicing your expectations to the team is of the utmost importance. I cannot tell you how many conversations I have with leaders who "assume" their team knows and understands their expectations. If you expect a certain behavior, then you need to clearly state it and hold people accountable, so everyone is on the same page. That is how you create a psychologically safe culture.

Creating a sense of belonging

Belonging is a crucial component of both individual and collective team performance. For your team to thrive, everyone must feel included. New team members or individuals who are somewhat different from the rest of the team may be at risk of feeling unintentionally excluded. That is simply due to human nature: We tend to gravitate towards people to whom we relate easily. This doesn't mean others are unimportant, but our unconscious actions can make them feel that way.

Inclusive and highly intuitive leaders intentionally assemble a diverse team with a wide range of perspectives. They recognize that this diversity fosters growth and enables the team to reach its full potential. These leaders actively challenge the team dynamics to encourage stretching and development.

Assembling a diverse team can contribute to a sense of belonging, as employees may appreciate knowing that other people share their background and look like them in the group. However, that step alone is not enough. Team-building activities are highly effective for fostering team cohesiveness by promoting reflection and encouraging team members to consider diverse perspectives. Tools I have successfully employed as both a team leader and a consultant—which are excellent for this purpose—include group coaching, interaction and communication games, perspective-building exercises, and custom role plays which I refer to as "Real Plays," which I will expand on later.

Taking steps to ensure everyone on your team feels a sense of belonging can improve your recruiting efforts. I've worked with some companies that have a very tenured workforce. Some have begun recruiting from other companies and industries to diversify their workforce and introduce new expertise and successful strategies. Sometimes the goal is to diversify an environment that is predominantly a particular demographic by bringing in highly qualified people from a different demographic.

While the strategy can work extremely well, it can also be undermined by unintended obstacles that ultimately work against the leader's goals. Team members' behaviors, such as leaving someone out of meetings, bullying, or targeting an employee with cutting remarks, can impact their ability to contribute. It is important, as a leader, to keep an eye out for these actions in your team. A telltale sign is if a new person in the role is not performing as you had hoped. Was it a bad hire? If that scenario is unlikely at their level, given the time and effort invested in the vetting process, it is probably an issue of conforming or not. Unfortunately, I see many leaders side with their long-tenured teams and expect a new person to innovate in a group that actively opposes change. Even talented leaders are not machines, and to foster the performance you want to see, you will need to set expectations that support them in shifting the culture. That can take a conscious and intentional approach.

Bringing mental health out of the shadows

Psychological safety is tied to another factor that shapes team members' experiences and actions: mental health. Feeling abused, neglected, overlooked, disrespected, or undervalued can not only erode psychological safety but also affect mental health. Someone who is experiencing any or all of these feelings may start to "go through the motions" to avoid bringing any attention to themselves and prevent the negative consequences of working in a psychologically unsafe environment.

A lack of belonging can exacerbate the impact on someone's mental health. When a team of people all think alike, that can be a challenging scenario for a newbie on the team, especially if they are different from the larger group. There is a lot they will need to overcome and do to conform and "fit in." Hopefully, that will not compromise their value system or personal comfort zone.

Individuals suppressing their true selves can experience a sense of disconnection and dissatisfaction that can lead to mental health issues over time. The constant struggle to fit in can lead to stress, anxiety, burnout, and mental trauma.

It is also a type of "emotional work" that can stifle personal growth. Arie Russel Hochschild introduced the concept of emotional labor in 1980 to describe the extra layer of responsibility that comes with trying to make others feel comfortable with us when we are different from them. Emotional labor often leads to what she calls "invisible mending."[5] This "involves carefully adjusting oneself to meet the unspoken demands of the workplace," she explained. "While the traditional definition of invisible mending refers to the delicate process of repairing clothing from the inside, ensuring that the fixes remain unseen, this version encapsulates the often-overlooked efforts employees invest in conforming to organizational norms—efforts that can come at a significant psychological cost."

There are many examples of this. For instance, many men of greater physical size know that they must be mindful of their communication style. If they are too passionate, they can be labeled as aggressive or intimidating. Another example of emotional labor I often hear about comes from women executives who work on predominantly male teams: If they assert themselves too much, they tend to be labeled as being aggressive and emotional, even though they are displaying the same behaviors as their male counterparts. This is not limited to women; it is often true for anyone "different" from the main group. The reactions they experience are sometimes a form of bias.

Conforming can create another toll on the individuals on your team: It can lead to missed opportunities to explore new interests, develop new skills, and pursue personal passions.[6] If you are not aware of the pressures someone faces to conform and the toll it may be taking on them, it may be hard to bring out their full potential.

Being mindful of these phenomena as an Inquisitive Leader can go a long way toward setting a different tone for your team and achieving peak performance as a group. For a team to be high performing, innovation is key. With innovation comes different schools of thought, experiences, and thinking outside of the box. Just remember that everyone's box looks different. Innovation will only flourish when everyone on your team feels comfortable opening their box in front of the larger group.

It is important to hire people who will challenge the status quo ("the way we always do things") to encourage innovation, creativity, and growth. This will help the entire team expand their thinking. At the same time, you need to maintain team cohesion, tapping into your intuition to identify and circumvent problems. Managing differences with care and attention can protect the group and its morale.

This takes time and effort, but many of the most celebrated business leaders in history understood that it is worthwhile. Steve Jobs was an authoritative leader who was very focused on what he was trying to accomplish. He embraced innovation and rewarded people for their ideas and contributions from all levels of the organization, actively removing barriers that would prevent this. He set a space at the table for everyone to contribute from their respective positions. He was by no means perfect but was a great example of someone who valued every member of the team. Without his Courageous Curiosity, we would not have the benefits of the Apple products that so many people enjoy today. Once your people know they are valued, it will be easier to stay aligned with the reason you are all working together, your shared Purpose. That will be our focus for the next chapter.

Key Takeaways:

- Most successes and failures in an organization come down to people.

- Understand each team member's preferred working style, strengths, and weaknesses to build on their unique strengths and potential.

- Psychological safety is important for every member of the team.

- What you tolerate, the team will tolerate. You set the tone for the culture.

- Create a culture of belonging and transparency.

CHAPTER 5

Understanding Purpose

Summary: To enhance team motivation, alignment and performance, cultivate a strong sense of purpose. The Inquisitive Leader's role is to determine if the team understands it's collective "why" and, if not, to make it clear and unite everyone around it. Employees who see how their work contributes to a larger goal, both for their team and for the organization as a whole, are more engaged, resilient, and effective.

Our company was gearing up to launch a new phone that would be a game-changer in the marketplace. We had to bring many moving parts together to make it successful and had focused all of our resources on the launch. We were facing unthinkable timelines, with information changing daily right up to the launch. In technology, you launch while learning—that's the nature of innovation.

It was not a stretch, or even a hardship, for everyone on my team to jump in headfirst into this whirlwind. We all knew our Purpose, from the front-line rep to the senior leader. Everyone was excited. We each had our assignment and were motivated to succeed. Thinking back still excites me. We were part of something historic in the technology evolution era. Many of us still keep in touch today, cheering each other on professionally.

That experience was one of many that taught me the importance of the fourth stage of The CAPPP Advantage™: Understanding Purpose. Purpose is the collective "why" of the team and the work each person does. When it's present, everyone on the team understands what they are doing and why.

Sometimes, galvanizing events make our purpose crystal clear. I was on vacation in Bermuda, getting ready to fly home, when I heard the news of the terrorist attacks that took place on Sept. 11, 2001. My colleagues showed up at their desks in Morristown, N.J., not realizing the meaning of their work would change forever. Employees in all positions transformed our office into a command center, supplying equipment to emergency personnel at the crash site in NYC. It was "all hands-on deck." No one complained. Everyone jumped in to help.

Other times, Understanding Purpose requires an active effort. As our industry matured, our culture shifted. The days when everyone played a direct role in the company's performance were gone. The organization became more matrixed, and it was less obvious how each person's work impacted the bottom line. Our excitement began to wane, and the connection between our performance both individually and as a team, and our Purpose was not as clear. The company was still a powerhouse and number one in the industry, but the employees felt different. Some no longer felt the connection to the excitement we experienced in the early days. Leaders had to intentionally reinforce our sense of Purpose to rekindle it.

Purpose-to-Performance

As you work to strengthen your team's Purpose, it helps to visualize how employee Purpose drives organizational performance.

The Purpose-to-Performance Model

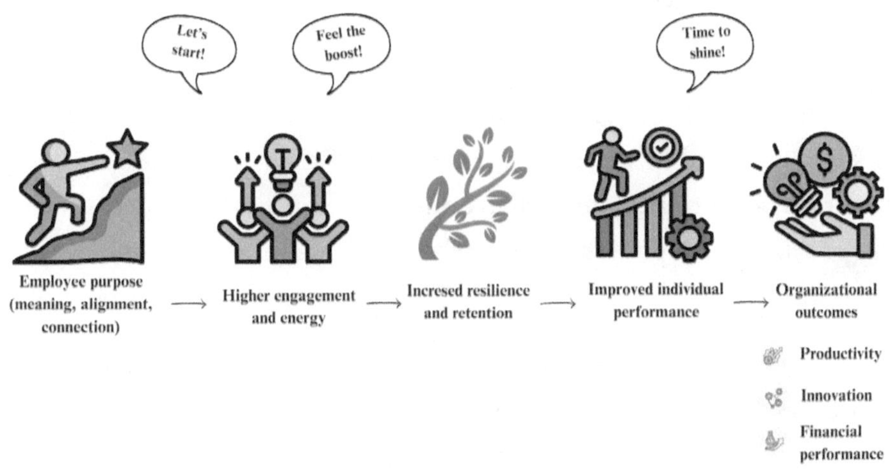

The CAPPP Advantage™ Purpose to Performance Model, developed by Frederica A. Peterson

Why Purpose matters

Taking the time to nurture your team's Purpose is one of the most powerful things you can do as an Inquisitive Leader. Purpose can be a multiplier. Harnessed correctly, it can allow a great team to emerge from a good one, and performance to reach new heights.

When employees see meaning in their work and align around a common goal, they are more engaged, resilient, and motivated. McKinsey research found that employees who feel their work fulfills their sense of purpose are two to five times more likely to report higher engagement, energy, and life satisfaction.[6] Purpose facilitates collaboration, better decision-making, and a unified workforce that can adapt to change more effectively. This translates into higher performance, lower turnover, and ultimately, stronger results.

Purpose also boosts performance directly. In one study, call center employees who were reminded of the real-world impact of their work (hearing success stories from beneficiaries) more than doubled their fundraising performance.[7] A shared sense of purpose can ultimately drive both innovation and organizational transformation.

A strong sense of purpose can also help in recruiting. Employees aligned with organizational Purpose report better health, higher resilience, and are significantly more likely to stay and recommend their workplace to others.[6]

All of this helps the bottom line: Companies with higher measures of employee Purpose and well-being outperform peers in return on assets, gross profit, and even stock performance.[8] However, Purpose must be authentic and clearly embedded in daily work practices to have its positive effect.[9]

How Inquisitive Leaders can nurture purpose

As an Inquisitive Leader, you should encourage individuals to understand the team's mission and see how their personal motivations and goals connect to it. Having a shared purpose provides direction and motivation and helps shape the team's collective identity and potential.

Revisiting a team's purpose quarterly during review periods or when assigning new projects helps team members understand how their work contributes to overarching organizational goals. Surprisingly, in most of the companies for which I've worked, the further down the organizational chart you go, the less teams comprehend how their work aligns with company performance goals. If leaders can get their teams aligned in purpose, teams will excel. As humans, we want to understand our roles. That understanding brings motivation, validation, and belonging.

Getting in touch with your collective purpose

With many of the groups I work with, structured activities are a quick and highly effective way to uncover and reinforce their shared purpose. One way to do this is through the Real Plays I mentioned earlier. These exercises, which I co-design with the client, are similar to a role play: Part of a story is provided to set the context for the topic at hand. It is usually a challenging situation that is familiar to the participants. Team members are asked to act out the outcome using their knowledge and skills. Once they have finished with the scenario, they discuss what they have observed and provide feedback based on learning objectives. A vast amount of observation goes into this activity, providing insights not possible through lectures. The outcomes are rich and promote genuine, actionable learning for the participants, allowing them to apply what they have learned throughout the session.

Sometimes, a Real Play exercise can uncover factors that are undermining a team's purpose. This happened when I was working with a team of more than 200 leaders in a research organization on an exercise focused on making assumptions. It wasn't easy to monitor the activity for the team, given how large it was and the fact that the exercise, including feedback, only lasts about 40 minutes.

The organization had been struggling a bit with embracing diversity, and, in wanting to do the right thing, was making minority employees feel a bit exploited. For instance, a black woman on the team was treated as the expert in anything that had to do with African Americans and ended up being the go-to person whenever anyone needed help understanding a situation involving Black employees. Adding to the mix was a top layer of senior leaders, many of them from military backgrounds, who had no tolerance for innovative thinking and processes. The strong desire for openness among newer employees and resistance from leadership left employees in the middle feeling stressed.

Doing a Real Play gave the leaders an inside look at how some on the team were feeling: isolated and excluded from fully contributing to team goals. Their lack of belonging was impacting their overall performance and their desire to stretch themselves more. This was revealed in an emotionally charged, life-changing "aha" moment, where they were able see through the "Real Play" how their behaviors were impacting the diverse employees. It became clear how unconscious biases and seemingly innocuous actions were leaving out and sometimes demeaning diverse employees.

When I performed this activity with another client, we uncovered resentments about the department's hiring of people from outside of the company. Because the company had been struggling to meet KPIs for the past few years, there had been a shake-up in senior leadership. With the change came the decision to diversify the teams with outside talent to bring new perspectives, innovative ideas, and experience to bring stronger performance. That was frustrating for many of the longtime employees, most of whom had been working together for decades. Many had assumed the positions would be filled internally, and they would at least have a shot at some of these roles.

It was also a very male-dominated organization, so the integration of new expertise and gender was a big shift from the previous culture. The legacy team members believed they were being welcoming, but their behavior did not align.

Ultimately, this exercise helped many of the leaders see the impact of their unconscious behaviors. More importantly, these exercises were done with everyone from the team, communicating what words alone could not.

In our discussions, we were able to connect these findings to the team's successes and failures in living its Purpose. If the team isn't aligned, performance suffers because we cannot fully leverage each individual's talent. Ultimately, the team achieved a cultural shift that made everyone more productive and effective in their work. Sometimes, we must go to uncomfortable places to get to "the zone of performance."

Key takeaways

When leaders do this well, purpose is no longer an abstract ideal—it becomes a lived experience that drives human potential, team performance and organizational success. As the leader, you cannot "give" employees a sense of purpose, but you can create the conditions where purpose thrives. This means:

- Show how everyday work ties into the bigger mission.

- Model authenticity and live the purpose in your own leadership behavior.

- Share stories of how the team's work makes a difference.

- Enable people, by allowing them to apply what they do best in ways that matter.

CHAPTER 6

Cultivating Performance

Summary: Exceptional performance emerges from Inquisitive Leadership, and the four preceding stages of The CAPPP Advantage™ framework —Building Connection and Rapport, Assessing the Team, Valuing People, and Understanding Purpose. Once you have created a workplace culture where team members are empowered and aligned around a powerful purpose, this alignment can propel both individual- and team-level outcomes and drive outstanding performance.

At one point in my career, I reached the point where I had achieved all I could in my role. Senior leaders decided to move some of us to lateral positions to gain broader experience leading in another organization within our region. I had the opportunity to take over a team that was not performing up to its potential. My primary focus was to get a full scope of the talent to help everyone improve their performance.

In retrospect, this was an opportunity to integrate all the key stages of The CAPPP Advantage™ framework. The first was to Build Connection and Rapport. I spent time meeting with each leader to understand their personal and professional journeys, what was working, what wasn't, and their vision for how we could work together for optimal results. Through these conversations, we began to establish a mutual respect and foundation for building a strong working relationship.

Next, I began to assess the team. I observed the behaviors and outcomes based on the expectations we agreed upon for the work. Each leader had a team of seven to ten people. One of the ways I assessed the leaders was through their ability to navigate the changes and newly established goals. What did they do well? What did they struggle with? What was motivating or demotivating for them? I used our one-on-one meetings to gain more clarity on some of the nuances in their behaviors and the root cause of any struggles.

Through Connecting and Assessing, I was able to establish a pretty strong grasp of each person's style and moved into Valuing People. Some of the leaders required more structure and detail. They needed to have a full understanding of any plan with timelines, milestones and resources. They were very focused on what their teams needed to meet the deliverables and execute according to the plan. Others needed to have more frequent meetings to talk through their understanding of current deliverables. There were a couple of individuals who naturally took the initiative to create standards of execution and updates that the rest of the team followed, and there were some who combined all these traits. Being observant and receptive to the unique communication and working preferences of my leaders was integral in building trust, confidence and engagement.

A big part of the work we had to focus on was Understanding Purpose. Team members were a bit misaligned in understanding their strategic purpose. They had a keen understanding of their tactical purpose, but they were underperforming against the other teams in the region. I concluded that as an organization, they lacked a shared purpose. The company did not make evident to each individual their value to the organization. As a result, team members only looked at their contributions in the context of the tasks they were given, when, in essence, they were the largest regional team, with the greatest customer footprint of all the other regions. What they did and how they did it mattered, but up to the time I came to work with them, it was not evident. They did their jobs to the best of their ability, but they had more to give.

When I assumed leadership of the team, I assessed that they were only working at fifty to sixty percent of their capacity, at best. Unlocking their capabilities required leaders to create a vision, provide a "why," show how each person on the team had a part in achieving the KPIs, and create a clear path in their performance agreements. That work was a heavy lift for my managers. They spent considerable time implementing, adjusting, and supporting our new vision. Nonetheless, I knew they were capable. Their belief turned into commitment, which turned into results, and it was contagious throughout the organization.

This team was one of the proudest achievements of my career. Doing the work in each of the stages led them from performing in last place to first place. After five years of working with them, our company was awarded the #1 position for the Association of Training and Development's (ATD) Top 10 training organizations that year. We won in part for a program created by one of my leaders. Even better, we heard that announcement live and received that award at the conference. It was a proud moment all around to be recognized in that room full of the top talent in our field, considering all the work we did to get there. Not only were we the number one team among our peers, but we were also the reason the company had secured the top honor that year. I was able to achieve such success with my team through Inquisitive Leadership using The CAPPP Advantage™ methodology.

Performance, the final stage of The CAPPP Advantage™ framework, emphasizes that high achievement isn't isolated. Instead, it stems directly from the environment a leader cultivates through the four prior stages. Building

Connection and Rapport, Assessing Your Team, Valuing People, and Understanding Purpose.

Collective efforts like this lead to powerful, high-performance outcomes. High performance is defined as consistently achieving and exceeding expectations, resulting in superior financial and non-financial results compared to competitors. It signifies not just short-term success, but sustained, exceptional results over time, encompassing financial goals, innovation, employee engagement, and overall organizational health.

Team-level outcomes

The first four stages of the Inquisitive Leadership model are designed to foster positive performance outcomes for your team, its individual members, and the entire organization. When implemented correctly, the framework can bring several potential positive outcomes for the group:

- **Increased engagement and morale**

  Leaders who show genuine curiosity and connect with their team members build trust. People feel seen and valued, which directly boosts their morale and their willingness to contribute.

  Example: Sarah, a team leader, asks individual team members what they are most proud of each week. This simple act of curiosity makes her team members feel seen and appreciated, contributing to a 25% increase in weekly project submissions and a palpable sense of positive energy in the office.

- **Enhanced psychological safety**

  By valuing each person and their unique perspective, you can create an environment where team members feel safe to speak up, share new ideas, and admit mistakes without fear of judgment. This is a critical ingredient for innovation.

  Example: Mark, a team lead, asks, "What's the riskiest idea you have for this project?" This question, posed without judgment, encourages a junior team member to propose a radical new marketing strategy. The team discusses it openly, leading to a major innovation in their campaign.

- **Greater resilience**

  A team that is deeply connected and aligned around a shared purpose is more adaptable and better equipped to handle challenges. It has the social capital and clarity of mission to navigate setbacks effectively.

  Example: When a key project deadline is missed, an Inquisitive Leader gathers the team and asks, "What did we learn from this?" rather than assigning blame. By focusing on learning and problem-solving, the team quickly identifies gaps in its processes and implements new strategies, positioning itself to hit the next project milestone ahead of schedule.

Team-Level Outcomes Model

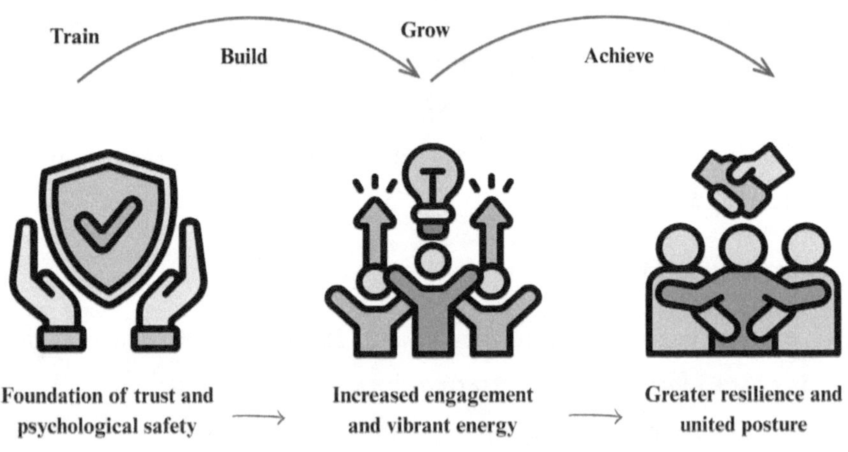

The CAPPP Advantage™ Team Outcomes Model, deevloped by Frederica A. Peterson

Individual-level outcomes

The first four stages of The CAPPP Advantage™ framework also bring about positive change for individual members of the team. Let's look at some of the potential outcomes.

- **Improved skill development**

  Inquisitive Leaders who accurately assess capabilities and ask probing questions can identify individual strengths and development areas more effectively. This leads to targeted growth opportunities and helps team members reach their full potential.

Example: An inquisitive manager notices that Jane, an employee, is a skilled communicator but struggles with data analysis. The manager asks, "What skills do you need to take on the next big challenge?" This question leads to a conversation about data literacy, and the manager enrolls Jane in a course on this, ultimately helping her advance to a new role.

- **Stronger autonomy and ownership**

When you align individuals with a shared Purpose, you empower them to take ownership of their work. They understand the "why" behind their tasks, which fosters a sense of responsibility and motivates them to deliver high-quality results.

Example: Instead of giving a team member a detailed list of tasks for a new feature, a leader asks, "How do you think we should approach this challenge to achieve our goal?" This question gives the employee the freedom to design the solution themselves, often resulting in a more creative and effective feature in which they feel personally invested.

- **Higher retention rates**

People who feel a strong connection to their team, a sense of purpose in their work and the confidence that their unique contributions are valued are far more likely to stay with the organization. This reduces turnover costs and preserves institutional knowledge.

Example: During a one-on-one meeting, a leader asks, "What is most meaningful to you in your work here?" When a valued employee, David, expresses a desire to work on a more Purpose-driven project, the leader reassigns him to a new initiative. David feels heard and valued, ultimately choosing to stay with the company despite receiving a competing offer.

Individual Level Outcomes Model

The CAPPP Advantage™
Individual Outcomes

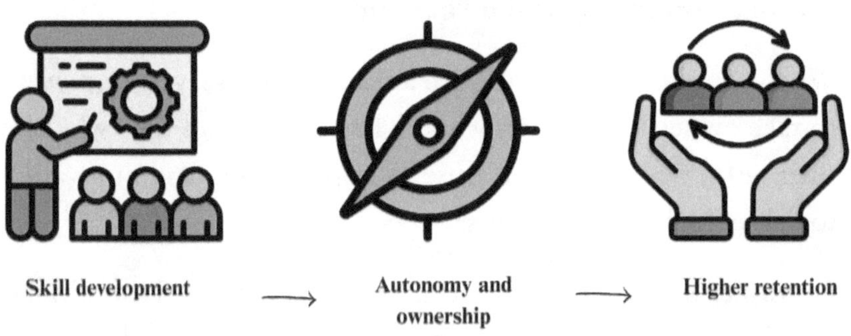

The CAPPP Advantage™ Individual Outcomes Model, developed by Frederica A. Peterson

Organizational outcomes

- **Increased innovation**

  Psychological safety and a deep understanding of team members' diverse capabilities create the ideal conditions for new ideas to emerge. People are more willing to experiment and take creative risks, which leads to breakthroughs.

  Example: A tech company's leadership team starts a new initiative where they regularly ask, "What customer problems are we not solving?" This simple question, posed to all levels of the organization, uncovers a widespread user frustration, leading to the development of a completely new product line that revolutionizes their market.

- **Improved productivity and efficiency**

When a team is aligned around a clear purpose, the group can work more efficiently. Everyone spends less time on misaligned tasks and more time on work that truly matters.

Example: A sales team leader asks, "What's one thing we can stop doing to be more effective?" The team collectively decides to eliminate an unnecessary weekly report. This frees up 10% of their time, which they can now dedicate to more impactful client interactions, boosting their sales numbers.

- **Enhanced financial performance**

All of these outcomes—from increased engagement to innovation and productivity—have a direct impact on the bottom line. High-performing teams are more likely to achieve and exceed their goals, driving greater profitability and success for the organization.

Example: A leader's consistent inquiry into what motivates employees leads to a highly engaged and resilient workforce. This team's productivity and low turnover result in a 15% increase in project delivery speed compared to other teams, directly translating to higher revenue for the business.

- **The Biggest Benefits of a High-Performing Team**

If you need to justify investments in the stages of Inquisitive Leadership, you can use the research that consistently demonstrates the advantages of high-performance teams, specifically in boosting productivity, fostering innovation, and increasing engagement.

- **Increased productivity and efficiency**

Research from Gallup consistently shows that engaged teams are more productive and profitable[10]. Their extensive studies have found that teams with high employee engagement rates achieve 21 percent higher profitability and 17 percent higher productivity. This is because engaged employees are more invested in their work and more likely to contribute discretionary effort, which directly translates to improved business outcomes.

- **Enhanced innovation and creativity**

The work of Dr. Amy Edmonson from Harvard Business School provides the foundation for this benefit. As we discussed in Chapter 2, research on psychological safety—the belief that a team environment is safe for interpersonal risk-taking—shows it is a critical driver of innovation Teams with high psychological safety are more willing to share creative, and sometimes half-formed, ideas, as well as admit mistakes. This open communication and learning mindset leads to more experimentation and, ultimately, greater innovation.

- **Improved employee engagement and retention**

Studies from organizations like Gallup and the Corporate Leadership Council confirm a strong link between team performance and employee retention[3]. Employees who feel a sense of connection and Purpose in their work are more likely to stay with a company. High-performing teams often foster this sense of belonging, as members are aligned on a shared mission and feel a strong sense of trust and support. This reduces turnover, saving the company significant costs associated with recruiting and training new employees.

Organizational Outcomes Model

The CAPPP Advantage™
Organizational Outcomes

The CAPPP Advantage™ Organizational Outcomes Model, developed by Frederica A. Peterson

Final takeaway: The Inquisitive Leader's high-performance formula

The Inquisitive Leader understands that high performance isn't a destination; it's a direct result of the intentional actions you take every day. As we've explored, the foundation of this journey lies in a simple yet profound truth: *Courageous Curiosity* is the catalyst for extraordinary results.

When you lead with questions rather than commands, you begin a powerful cascade that moves from the individual to the entire organization:

- You build trust and psychological safety (Chapter 1), which makes your team more *resilient* and fuels open communication.

- You accurately assess individual capabilities (Chapter 2), which empowers people to take ownership of their work and drives their *skill development*.

- You value each person for who they are (Chapter 3), which creates a sense of *belonging* and boosts engagement and retention.

- You align everyone around a shared Purpose (Chapter 4), which unites all efforts and clears the path for true *productivity* and efficiency.

Ultimately, the *Inquisitive Leadership* Model is your formula for success. By committing to these four inquisitive actions, you're not just creating a pleasant workplace; you're actively forging a high-performance team that is more innovative, productive, and resilient—and you are building a legacy of leadership that leaves your organization stronger than you found it.

AFTERWORD

Inquisitive Leadership leaders who already run their teams with high levels of engagement and transparency have already experienced the results. However, given the lack of emphasis on traditional communication and connection in the workplace today, there is an opportunity for *Inquisitive Leadership* to bring greater value than ever before. Younger generations in the workforce don't always understand the importance of actual human connection in the way that their older counterparts do. Body language conveys about 60 percent of what we mean when we speak with other people, so we need to rekindle face-to-face connection and conversation.

This is a human-first approach that will help you do that, and it is very different from the strategy-first approach most organizations use. If you don't have a healthy culture firmly established, your strategy will never work, no matter how much you want it to.

Building a great culture has become more complicated now that AI has entered the mix. With many AI tools now taking the place of actual leaders coaching their teams, applying the principles of *Inquisitive Leadership* is even more important than in the past. Nothing will ever take the place of the intuitive capabilities of the human psyche. What truly connects us as human beings is emotions, and that is the difference between man and machine. Although most organizations would tell you that emotions have no place in the office, that is old school thinking my friends, as emotions are what connect us.

Consider this: When you follow a leader, it is not because of the strategy they build, but rather their vision, that's a big difference. To cast a vision, you must first be able to feel it so that others believe it. Contrary to popular belief, we do not make decisions based on facts and logic alone. Those things inform us. We actually make decisions based on emotions.[12]

Consider how animal rescue organizations raise funds. Logically, we know that the shelters in our area need our support. If you find a stray in your neighborhood, you will want to have access to a shelter to ensure the animal gets properly housed and fed until they can find suitable pet parents. However, we often don't donate until we see commercials filled with pictures of malnourished animals. Why? Because we are being pulled into the situation emotionally by the images we are seeing.

Or think about the documentaries and crime podcasts you've seen that have brought injustices to light or caused serious uproars in our society. We may have read about the crimes they feature or seen the news stories, but when we watch or listen to the full account, we are suddenly moved to action. This is an example of the emotional drivers behind decision-making.

Now, what moves us in a business setting is rarely as dramatic as those commercials and films. However, the impact is very real. You're not likely to get a budget increase approved for your department if you can't get your senior leaders on board with the vision, or even better, feel the need behind it. Questions like, "What happens if we don't act?" or "What is the real impact?" are what move decisions forward..

As an Inquisitive Leader, you understand the impact of your actions because you've taken the time to learn to, ask the right questions, and come up with compelling answers with your team. *Courageous Curiosity* has the power to change outcomes, organizations, and profit margins.

Don't take your presence lightly. You cannot be replaced. An everyday leader who just worries about checks and balances needs to justify their role because any AI-based program can perform routine work. An Inquisitive Leader who understands the unspoken nuances of how to tap into and lead performance through curiosity, intuition, and transparency...well, that is the game changer and your ticket to remaining relevant in your work. Here's to your *Courageous Curiosity*, the gift that keeps on giving.

CONTINUE THE MOVEMENT

Leadership is not a title. It is a decision.

If this book stirred something in you —
let it become practice.

Inquisitive Leadership is the foundation of **The CAPPP Advantage™ Performance Model** — a disciplined framework designed to strengthen leadership capability, increase retention, and drive sustained high performance.

Through enterprise and small business partnerships, certifications, diagnostics, and executive intensives, leaders transform curiosity into measurable impact.

This is not about leading softly.
It is about leading with depth courage and intention.

If you are ready to cultivate high performance fueled by curiosity,
continue the journey.

Explore programs, certifications, and partnerships at:
www.FredericaPeterson.com

**The future of leadership will be written by those who dare to ask
better questions.**

MEASURE WHAT MATTERS

Introducing The CAPPP Advantage™ Leadership Assessment

Insight creates awareness.
Measurement creates growth.

As a reader of *Inquisitive Leadership*, you now have access to The CAPPP Advantage™ Leadership diagnostic tool — a structured assessment used to evaluate leadership capability across five drivers of sustained high performance:

Building Connection and Rapport
Assessing the Team
Valuing People
Understanding Purpose
Cultivating Performance

Scan the code below to access the assessment.

Enter your name and email to receive the assessment and your personalized leadership profile.

93

Your information is treated with respect and confidentiality and will not be shared.

Leadership is shaped by the questions we are willing to ask.

Appendix I: Why connection matters: What researchers have discovered

A significant body of research and psychological theory explains why it is important for leaders to have strong connections with their team members. Managers account for up to 70 percent of the variance in employee engagement, according to research by Gallup[13]. When leaders recognize, support, and connect with their people on a human level, employees are more likely to stay, contribute more, and bring their best ideas forward.

The quality of leader–team member relationships, often described as *Leader–Member Exchange (LMX)*, is one of the most studied predictors of workplace outcomes. A meta-analysis by Ilies, Nahrgang, and Morgeson[14] found that strong LMX relationships lead to better communication, higher cooperation, and increased performance. Likewise, Gerstner and Day (1997) concluded that employees with high-quality relationships with their leaders experience greater job satisfaction, perform better, and are more likely to remain with the organization.[15]

The impact extends beyond performance. Research by Kelloway and Barling (2010) shows that supportive leadership can reduce employee stress and burnout[16], while Carmeli, Reiter-Palmon, and Ziv (2010) found that inclusive leadership—where leaders actively invite contribution and create a sense of belonging—significantly boosts creativity and innovation.[17]

In essence, relationship-based leadership is not just about being liked—it's about creating the conditions for people and organizations to thrive. Trust leads to engagement, engagement leads to performance, and performance sustains both innovation and retention.

Understanding Leader-Member Exchange (LMX) Theory

Leader-Member Exchange Theory is perhaps the most central and widely researched concept that directly addresses the quality of the relationship between a leader and individual team members, so it can be helpful to understand it in further depth.

- Core idea: LMX theory posits that leaders do not treat all subordinates the same. Instead, they develop unique, dyadic (two-person) relationships with each team member. These relationships can range from high-quality (in-group) to low-quality (out-group).[18]

- High-quality LMX: Relationships that fit this description are characterized by high levels of trust, respect, mutual obligation, open communication, shared understanding, and going "above and beyond" formal job descriptions.

- Benefits of High LMX: Research consistently shows that high-quality LMX relationships are associated with numerous positive outcomes, including:

  * Higher job satisfaction: Employees in high LMX relationships report greater happiness with their jobs.[19]

  * Increased organizational commitment: Team members feel a stronger bond with the organization.

* Improved job performance: Both objective performance ratings and subjective perceptions of performance are higher.[20]

* Greater psychological empowerment: Employees feel more control over their work and find it more meaningful.

* Reduced intention to quit: Employees are less likely to leave the organization.

* Enhanced organizational citizenship behaviors (OCBs): Employees are more willing to engage in behaviors that benefit the organization but are not formally rewarded (e.g., helping colleagues, volunteering).

* Increased innovation and creativity: Psychological safety fostered by high LMX encourages risk-taking and idea-sharing.[21]

* Lower stress and burnout: The support and trust in these relationships act as buffers against workplace stressors.

REFERENCES

1. Louis Cozolino, *The Neuroscience of Human Relationships: Attachment and the Developing Social Brain*, (New York: W.W. Norton & Company, 2014).

2. Paul J. Zak, *Behavioral and Brain Sciences* , Volume 28 , Issue 3 , June 2005 , pp. 368 - 369; Paul J. Zak, "The Neurobiology of Trust," Scientific American Magazine, Vol. 298 No. 6, June 2008.

3. Amy C. Edmondson, "Psychological Safety and Learning Behavior in Work Teams, " *Administrative Science Quarterly*, vol. 44, no. 2, June 1999, pp. 350–383.

4. Kishore, Borra "The Importance of Getting to Know Your Team Members", LinkedIn, Feb. 19., 2022.   https://www.linkedin.com/pulse/importance-getting-know-your-team-members-kishore-borra/

5. Janelle E. Wells and Doreen MacAulay, D. "Invisible mending: The silent struggle of conforming at work," *Psychology Today*, Aug. 12, 2024. https://www.psychologytoday.com/us/blog/our-invisible-work/202408/invisible-mending-the-silent-struggle-of-conforming-at-work#:~:text=A%20workplace%20culture%20that%20implicitly,talent%20and%20increased%20recruitment%20costs.

6. McKinsey & Co. *Help your employees find purpose—or watch them leave, 2021*. https://www.mckinsey.com/capabilities/people-and-organizational-performance/our-insights/help-your-employees-find-purpose-or-watch-them-leave

7. Adam Grant, "The significance of task significance: Job performance effects, relational mechanisms, and boundary conditions," *Journal of Applied Psychology, 93*(1), 2008, 108–124. https://selfdetermination-theory.org/SDT/documents/2008_Grant_JAP_TaskSignificance.pdf

8. Insiders Studio with Indeed, "Beyond the obvious, here are the business benefits of investing in employee wellbeing," *Business Insider*, Sept. 17, 2024. https://www.businessinsider.com/sc/here-are-the-business-benefits-of-investing-in-employee-wellbeing Insiders

9. Durand, R., & Huynh, T. (2024). *What is the purpose of purpose?* Organization Theory, 5(1), 1–22. https://doi org/10.1177/27550311241283390

10. Gallup Inc. *State of the global workplace: 2020 report*, Washington, D.C.: Gallup Press, 2020.

11. Corporate Leadership Council, "Driving employee performance and retention through engagement," New York City: Corporate Executive Board, 2004.

12. Gardiner Morse, "Decisions and Desire," Harvard Business Review, Jan. 2006. https://hbr.org/2006/01/decisions-and-desire.

13. Gallup, *State of the Global Workplace: 2023 Report, Washington, D.C.:* Gallup, Inc., 2023.

14. R. Ilies, J.D., J. D. Nahrgang and F.P. Morgeson, F. P., "Leader–member exchange and citizenship behaviors: A meta-analysis," *Journal of Applied Psychology, 92*(1), 2007, pp. 269–277.

15. C. R. Gerstner, and D. V. Day, "Meta-analytic review of leader–member exchange theory: Correlates and construct issues," *Journal of Applied Psychology, 82*(6), 1997, pp. 827–844.

16. E.K. Kelloway and J. Barling, J., "Leadership development as an intervention in occupational health psychology," *Work & Stress, 24*(3), 2010, pp. 260–279.

17. A. Carmeli, R. Reiter-Palmon and E. Ziv, "Inclusive leadership and employee involvement in creative tasks in the workplace: The mediating role of psychological safety," *Creativity Research Journal, 22*(3), 2010, pp. 250–260.

18. G.B. Graen and M. Uhl-Bien, "Relationship-based approach to leadership: Development of Leader–Member Exchange (LMX) theory of leadership over 25 years," *Leadership Quarterly, 6*(2), 1995, pp. 219–247.

19. R. D. Hackett, J.-L, Farh, L.J. Song and L.M. Lapierre, L. M. "LMX and job satisfaction: A meta-analysis," *Journal of Occupational and Organizational Psychology, 76*(3), 2003, pp. 341–356.

20. B. Erdogan and J. Enders, "Support from the top: Supervisors' perceived organizational support as a moderator of leader–member exchange to satisfaction and performance relationships," *Journal of Applied Psychology, 92*(2), 2003, pp. 321–330.

21. R. Basu and S.G. Green, S. G. "Leader–Member Exchange and Transformational Leadership: An empirical examination of innovative behaviors in leader–member dyads," *Journal of Applied Social Psychology,* *27*(6), 1997, pp. 477–499.

ABOUT THE AUTHOR

Frederica Peterson is an award-winning executive coach, leadership consultant, and the Founder of Frederica Peterson Consulting, LLC. With more than two decades of leadership and advisory experience, she partners with enterprise organizations to cultivate high-performance cultures through curiosity-driven leadership.

She is the creator of **The CAPPP Advantage™ Performance Model**—a practical, research-informed framework designed to elevate leadership capability, strengthen retention, and drive sustained high performance. Her work challenges leaders to replace control with inquiry, assumption with assessment, and compliance with commitment.

Frederica has advised leaders and teams at organizations including Accenture, CNN, Facebook, Prudential, Honeywell, NASA, the National Basketball Association, and the United States Department of Homeland Security. Prior to launching her firm, she held leadership roles at Verizon Wireless and KPMG, where she was recognized with multiple company and industry awards for her impact and innovation.

A respected voice on inclusive and high-impact leadership, Frederica is known for her ability to ask the questions others avoid—and to help leaders become comfortable with the discomfort required for growth.

Through her work, she equips leaders at every level to unlock potential, build meaningful connection, and create the conditions where people and performance thrive.

NOTES

NOTES

NOTES

NOTES

NOTES

NOTES

NOTES

NOTES

NOTES

NOTES

NOTES

114

www.ingramcontent.com/pod-product-compliance
Lightning Source LLC
Chambersburg PA
CBHW021331060726
47591CB00006B/1978